These hearty whole-food recipes cover all meals of the day, from power breakfasts and quick lunches to satisfying dinners, one-pot meals, and sweet treats. With high-protein recipes and tips and ingredient swaps for a wide range of nutritional needs, *Vegan Wholesome* provides the framework to enjoy comforting plant-based meals while also meeting your daily protein goals.

ENJOY DISHES LIKE

Sweet Jalapeño Cornbread Waffles

Tim's Greek Salad with Homemade Feta

Creamy Gochujang Chickpeas
and Lentils with Poblano Pepper

Teriyaki Orzo Casserole

Jackfruit Pinto Bean Chili

Protein Packed Mac 'n' Cheese

Smoky Bean Dip

Chocolate Pots de Crème

vegan
wholesome

vegan wholesome

high-protein meals
and snacks to
energize and nourish

Brandi Doming

RODALE
NEW YORK

By Brandi Doming

The Vegan 8
Vegan Wholesome

Published in the United States by RODALE BOOKS,
an imprint of RANDOM HOUSE, a division of
PENGUIN RANDOM HOUSE LLC, NEW YORK.

RODALE and the Plant colophon are registered trademarks of
PENGUIN RANDOM HOUSE LLC.

LIBRARY OF CONGRESS CATALOGING-IN-PUBLICATION DATA
Names: Doming, Brandi, author.
Title: Vegan wholesome / BRANDI DOMING.
Description: First edition. | New York, NY: Rodale, [2025] |
    Includes index.
Identifiers: LCCN 2024012602 (print) | LCCN 2024012603
    (ebook) | ISBN 9780593797433 (hardcover) | ISBN
    9780593797440 (ebook)
Subjects: LCSH: Vegan cooking. | Cooking (Natural foods) |
    LCGFT: Cookbooks.
Classification: LCC TX837 .D625 2025 (print) | LCC TX837 (ebook)
    | DDC 641.5/6362--dc23/eng/20240327
LC record available at https://lccn.loc.gov/2024012602
LC ebook record available at https://lccn.loc.gov/2024012603

Printed in China

RodaleBooks.com | RandomHouseBooks.com

9 8 7 6 5 4 3 2 1

First Edition

Book design by SONIA PERSAD

For you, Mom.

You always told me it's just as easy to dream big as it is to dream small, so why not dream big? It all starts with a thought. You helped me to see that thoughts can lead to dreams coming true. You showed me to not limit myself by my own thoughts. Your belief in me and help throughout this book I will forever be grateful for. I love you endlessly, Mom, and couldn't have finished this book without your love and support. I miss you deeply and every single moment of every day.

To my biggest fan, Dad.

You have always been so proud of me and made me feel so special. You are the wisest, most compassionate, and most loving man I've ever known. I know things are so different now with you and Alzheimer's, and you don't understand much anymore. This breaks my heart, but you feel and still give love like you always have even if you can't verbalize it anymore. I know you would be so proud of this book I've created, and I dedicate it to you and Mom for always loving me and believing in me.

contents

my story 8

chapter 1   **first power meals of the day**   25

chapter 2   **impressive sides and appetizers**   49

chapter 3   **fast and fabulous lunches**   75

chapter 4   **casseroles you'll crave**   99

chapter 5   **soul-satisfying soups**   121

chapter 6   **wholesome and hearty mains**   155

chapter 7   **sweet and savory snacks**   191

chapter 8   **feel-good desserts**   213

chapter 9   **go-to sauces, spices, and staples**   241

acknowledgments   279

index   282

my story

My journey to writing this book has been full of lots of highs and lows over the past few years. When I released my first book in 2018, my goal was to release another one not too long after that. However, due to many challenges in my personal life, that did not happen. I was married at the time and a full-time mom to my daughter, Olivia. I was trying to juggle raising her, running my blog, and being a wife. I faced many challenges in my marriage in those years that I kept hidden from everyone else. I did not share anything with my family or close friends. I didn't reveal what I was facing until the year I filed for divorce, which was in 2021. I was severely depressed for a couple of years leading up to that time. I felt lost and hopeless and finally turned to my amazing parents and friends for guidance and support. My dad and mom were crucial to helping me find my way. My dad was my rock.

Before I filed, I was struggling so much that I knew I had to find a way to deal with my situation and depression. During 2021 I started lifting weights and dancing daily in my room as a way of coping. I have always been involved in exercising on and off for years, but I had really neglected it. With my depression, I knew that I had to finally commit to sticking with a fitness routine because I knew the benefits were not just physical, but also mental. I started lifting weights five or six days a week and did not waver. I found it helped me to feel a lot better and it was a personal time that I truly looked forward to every day. Since I was rather sad about what was going on personally, the workouts helped take my mind off everything. At this same time, I started eating healthier and cutting out my daily sweets and replacing them with fruit protein smoothies. My body composition started changing and I felt better physically and mentally. My marriage was the next big change I made.

> **it was a personal time that I truly looked forward to every day.**

After filing for divorce, the lifelong dream I had to become a ballroom dancer started flooding my mind and heart so strongly, I couldn't stop thinking about it daily. I was afraid to make that commitment though. I was afraid of the unknown and that I'd embarrass myself or not have the ability to be as great as I dreamed to be in my mind. But one day I finally realized that my dream was instilled in my heart for a reason. That yearning and passion I always had for dancing was not meant to be stifled or ignored any longer. I knew it was God opening that doorway for me to finally pursue it. I also knew, since I was finally single, that nothing and nobody could now stop me. I made the call and my life changed drastically in every wonderful way possible.

I started my dance journey with Fred Astaire Dance Studios in Cypress, Texas, in February 2022. The first person I met when I walked through the doors would completely change my life. This amazing man from Hungary named Richárd Kaszás, known as "Richie," listened to my story, grabbed my hand, and walked me out onto the dance floor for my first lesson. From that day forward, he has listened to me cry and scream with excitement, and has guided me toward my dance dreams. Not only has he taught me the technical side of ballroom dancing, but he has listened to my desires and dreams as a dancer and embraced them all. He truly is a master and an amazing human, as well as my friend. Both he and his amazing Greek wife, Foteini Pangea, known as "Faith," have been a huge part of my journey.

Shortly after meeting Richie, I met my other teacher, Tilemachos Fatsis, known as "Tim." Tim is from Greece and if you follow me on social media, you've seen how goofy our relationship is. Just like Richie, there are not enough words to describe how much he means to me and how much he has also helped to guide me and mold me into a ballroom dancer. The joy, excitement, and hilarious energy that he always brings when we dance together is unmatched. Thanks to Tim and Richie, I know how to dance the rumba, cha-cha, salsa, bachata, East Coast swing, hustle, waltz, Viennese waltz, tango, Argentine tango, and foxtrot! Literally, I'm living my dreams to be able to dance all of these styles.

My third teacher is Barnabas Vadon, also from Hungary. I strictly take bachata lessons with him and I refer to him as my fun teacher. Bachata is not part of the competitions that I train for with Tim and Richie, but rather for entertainment shows. I absolutely love bachata and am so grateful to have Barnabas as my teacher. He is always making me laugh, is a wonderful friend, so passionate, and we have amazing chemistry. Since dance is such a huge part of my life, it was important to me to honor them by sharing who they are and creating a recipe inspired by each of them—Hungarian Bean Soup (page 143), Tim's Greek Salad with Homemade Feta (page 66), and Hungarian Sült Polenta Margherita (page 109).

my life changed drastically in every wonderful way possible.

Pictured with my dance teacher Richárd Kaszás

Learning how to ballroom dance ultimately led to my first judged competition after just seven months of lessons and I earned a first-place medal. To reach this lifelong dream, after going through depression and a huge life transition and thinking that it would never come true, I realized that anything can truly happen in this life if you fight for it. I share my personal struggles with my readers because I know life can be quite painful and you can feel hopeless. It helps when you know you are not alone. My goal from day one when I started my blog was always to help people. It was through sharing healthier recipes, of course, but over time that has grown into sharing my personal life changes with you all, as well as integrating fitness and posting my workouts because of how important I believe exercise is to mental health.

So many of us struggle when we don't show ourselves self-love. Part of loving ourselves is taking care of our bodies through food choices, committing to exercising, as well as following our passions. All of these components play an important role in finding joy and a balanced life. I spent so many years taking care of others and neglecting myself. It left me feeling so empty and heartbroken. Never again will I neglect myself like that. Sharing my dance journey and the fitness side of my life, in addition to my recipes, on social media is what ultimately led to this book, which focuses on so many wonderful high-protein recipes. Over the last few years, many of you started embracing fitness and dance into your own lives and started requesting a high-protein cookbook. My hope is that

each of you feels my heart through my words, my passion through these delicious recipes, and finds health and nourishment from this book. I hope it becomes a staple in your kitchen and that you enjoy it for many years to come.

my first book, *the vegan 8*

Many of you amazing readers have been following my blog, The Vegan 8, for many years (some since the very beginning over a decade ago!). Many of you also have my first cookbook, *The Vegan 8*, which was dedicated to recipes only featuring 8 ingredients, not counting salt, pepper, or water (or optional ingredients). This 8-ingredient approach was the theme of my blog for many, many years, but I stopped writing "8 ingredient only" recipes back in 2020. After creating recipes for so long and gaining such a loyal following who love my style and flavor-packed recipes, I wanted to branch out and allow my creativity to fully expand, not feel limited. There have always been certain types of recipes that I've wanted to create for you, but could not because of the 8 ingredients maximum. I kept the Vegan 8 name because that is what I'm known for and I still have hundreds of recipes on my website featuring 8-ingredient (or less) recipes.

When I made the announcement, I was thrilled to hear from so many of you that, while you appreciated the short-ingredient recipes, you were simply a fan of my recipes and how easy they were. I heard repeatedly that you didn't mind at all that I was no longer sticking to the short-ingredient recipes and that you just wanted me sharing my recipes, period, with all of you.

Because of you, the transition to my newer recipes has been smooth sailing. I still make sure that my recipes are top-notch, packed full of flavor, and of course, easy. It has allowed me to feel completely content in my creative kitchen and this book is no exception. This book represents my best recipes yet! Everything in this book is so incredibly full of flavor, with uncomplicated steps and magical results. I'm so excited to share this book with you. I felt so creative in my kitchen and ecstatic at the deliciousness on my lips as I tested all these recipes for you.

You will still find that the recipes are simple, not overwhelming, and that the extra ingredients are typically just spices and flavor enhancers. While they're still super easy, they're even more flavorful! I hope you love these recipes as much as the amazing taste testers who helped me through this process and I do.

my eating philosophy

Meals need to be satiating, rich in flavor, and keep me full. Combining the right foods together creates a happy palate, as well as prevents hunger too soon after a meal. This is really important to me on a daily basis. I don't like meals that I eat and then feel hungry again after an hour. I've tried doing low-carb and even low-fat diets in the past and both left me feeling miserable and

protein

+

a high-calorie starchy complex carb

+

a low-calorie nonstarchy carb

+

a fat

constantly hungry. I learned that for me to truly feel healthy and happy, there should be a combination of multiple foods to include the benefits of each macronutrient (often referred to as macros), which are protein, carbohydrates, and fat.

The best way to do this is to combine a protein, a high-calorie starchy complex carb, a low-calorie nonstarchy carb, and a fat. This combined balance of all the macronutrients adds nutritional benefits and keeps you feeling satiated. You will learn more about how to do this in How to Build Meals (page 22).

In between meals, I find a snack is needed on some days, depending on my activity level. In other words, I don't eat snacks daily. When it comes to desserts, I do not eat them daily either. I crave savory much more than sweets these days and prefer to have just a few bites of a dessert. I find that satisfies me perfectly.

For post-workouts I like to drink My Go-to Protein Berry Smoothie (page 34). If you are pressed for time, the smoothie definitely can count as breakfast!

This is my basic eating philosophy and how I like to eat. Of course, life is unpredictable and my days are not all the same. On days I eat out or am out of town, I don't stress about the perfect meal or macronutrients. I like to enjoy my life, as well as food, so I never allow perfection to override my love for food.

Many years ago I trained and competed in a figure competition, and the pressure and stress of preparing for it had me hyperfocused on every single thing I ate. I stressed about each carb, every gram of fat, and each calorie. I was absolutely miserable and it made me realize that was not something that I wanted to be involved with at all. I also found I lost way more weight than I wanted, and lost my breasts and curves, which affected my confidence in how I looked. I have a lot of respect for the people who compete and are dedicated to it, but after just one competition, I never wanted to be counting my calories on a day-to-day basis.

So, while nutrition stats (per serving unless otherwise specified) are included for the recipes in this book for your convenience, I personally do not count calories anymore. I know, through experience, how to combine meals, but have let go of counting the exact calories and percentage of each macronutrient that some people like to do with their diet. So I do not push counting calories in this book, but rather give you a general guideline. Mental health is just as important as physical health, in my opinion.

Regardless of what some people think of a vegan diet, it's way more satisfying than boring salads or never-ending smoothies. I love to show people that vegans still eat pizza, decadent pasta dishes, tacos, comforting stews and soups, and even amazing desserts. They're just made without meat and dairy, but the recipes I share in this book will not have you missing the meat or cheese. This book will show you just how delicious and fulfilling a vegan diet is.

vegan wholesome

If you've been a follower of mine for a while, you know that most of my recipes focus on healthier ingredients, no added oils, and no store-bought cheeses or fake meats. I do eat these sometimes, as I'm not about perfection, but I try to share healthier, more wholesome ingredients, which you'll find in this book. Most of these processed cheeses and meats or premade meals are full of oils, sodium, and additives that can be harmful over time. I use nondairy yogurt for a few recipes in this book, because of the amazing tang it adds to recipes, but there are some great, healthy yogurts available that don't contain nearly as many processed ingredients as the cheeses and meats. If you wish to avoid store-bought yogurt, you can always use a homemade yogurt! None of the recipes in this book rely on any vegan butters or added oils, but use whole-food fats like nuts, seeds, and avocado instead.

These recipes will give you energy, keep you full, nourish you, and satisfy your tummies in a fantastic way!

hearty meals

This book contains more savory and hearty meals and entrées than my first book, which was heavy on desserts and sweets. One of the requests I received from many of you who bought my first book was more meals to choose from! So I delivered big-time for you! This book has a large chapter of mains for quick dinners and lunches, and a casserole section. Let's not forget all the soups as well. You will have so many options every week to make delicious meals for your family! Some of my very favorites are the Protein-Rich BBQ Sesame Tofu Bites (page 202) in the Snacks chapter, the Protein-Packed Mac 'n' Cheese (page 162), and the Hungarian Bean Soup (page 143). These crowd-pleasers are all very filling and satisfying.

cooking without oil

For over a decade, I've been sharing recipes without using oil. Nowadays, I use it on special occasions where I feel an oil or vegan butter tastes best—like in classic frosting, or sesame oil, where only a tiny amount is needed for a huge flavor impact—and sometimes call for nonstick spray in my recipes. My belief is that life is short, and we shouldn't be so consumed or stressed out by the idea of eating perfectly. I tried that in the past and it was not healthy for me mentally and caused more stress than the "negative" side effects of said oil. I learned to let go of perfection so I could enjoy my food. Now, when I go out to eat, I don't worry about oil in my food.

For the recipes in this book, I avoided using oil and stuck to whole-food fats. Why? Well, simply, whole-food fats like nuts, seeds, and avocados contain all the macronutrients (protein, carbs, and fat) in the whole food. But in oil, all the nutrition like protein and carbs have been removed and you are left with nothing but 100 percent pure liquid fat. So oil is not only the most calorie-dense food, but also very easy to overconsume. The majority of oils contain 14 grams of fat in just 1 tablespoon. A tablespoon of nut butter, by comparison, is 8 to 9 grams of fat. That is closer to half. The Dietary Guidelines for Americans recommends that 20% to 35% of total calories for the day come from fats. Think about how much oil is used in normal cooking—a few tablespoons here and there and you end up with A LOT of extra fat at each meal. Traditional salad dressing recipes usually call for ¼ to ½ cup of oil. That is a ton of oil! Since I rarely cook with oils, my recipes are saving a lot of calories and fat compared to traditional recipes.

I don't want you to worry, though. Many of my readers have been making my oil-free recipes for years and they will attest to nothing lacking. My recipes are well-seasoned and full of flavor and texture. I do include fat, just in its whole-food form instead of oil.

So, keep in mind that I do not avoid fats whatsoever, nor do I believe in a fat-free diet. I just try to limit using strictly oils as my fat sources. Fat-free and oil-free can confuse a lot of people, so this information should make it easier to understand now.

To sauté without oil, you will need a good-quality nonstick pan. Since oil is not used, a traditional stainless steel pan will be more challenging, as veggies will stick to it or burn easily. I usually cook my veggies with either water or broth over medium heat. For example, to sauté onions, add ¼ cup water to a pan over medium heat. Once the water is simmering, add the onions and stir occasionally until translucent.

Water will cook away much more quickly than oil, so you will want to keep an eye on it. Add more water as needed, just to prevent sticking or burning. You can cook them until translucent, 5 to 8 minutes, or 10 to 15 minutes to caramelize them. Stir them constantly with very little water to caramelize. Do not walk away or they will burn. Add a pinch of salt for delicious caramelized onions!

weighing ingredients

Just like in my first book, it's important to weigh ingredients, following the gram weights I've listed. Invest in a kitchen scale. They are inexpensive and you can find them at grocery stores or online. I bought mine on Amazon and I have used it for years. If you haven't used one before, it may seem odd at first, but within a few days you will love it! Not only will it produce the intended results as I've written, but it will make cooking so much easier and quicker than getting out measuring cups.

Weighing ingredients is mostly important when working with flours, like batters for pancakes or cakes that will be baked. When measuring flours with measuring cups, no two people will measure the same and this leaves a lot of room for error. With flours, being off by just 2 tablespoons can affect results. This is even more true for vegan, gluten-free, and oil-free recipes like mine. I meticulously test my recipes for accuracy. Since they are oil-free, the accuracy is even more important. Oils not only provide

moisture, but they also provide structure in a baked good. So, by not using oil, there is a greater chance that the recipe will turn out dry and crumbly. Since my recipes are mostly gluten-free and oil-free, each ingredient plays a vital role in its moisture and structure. Swapping out ingredients or mismeasuring can easily affect the result.

You will come to love the accuracy you get each time you make a recipe. I know this because over the years I've converted thousands of my readers into kitchen scale users. The only thing you don't want to rely on the kitchen scale for is really small amounts like teaspoons, as the scale can't accurately measure such small weights, and that can mess up the recipe. So, it's best to use measuring spoons for small amounts like spices.

kitchen tools and soaking cashews

In non-vegan recipes, dairy is used to achieve richness and creaminess. In order to obtain similar results in vegan recipes, cashews and other nuts or seeds are used. However, since nuts are hard, they require a high-powered blender or strong food processor to blend them until completely smooth. Once they are blended up fully, they serve a role similar to dairy.

You'll find that I blend cashews in many of my recipes to add creaminess, but if you're not working with a high-powered blender, it's important to soak the cashews beforehand. To soak cashews, add them to a bowl and fill with warm water. Leave them

to soak at room temperature for 6 hours or overnight. This will make them much softer and easier to blend. Drain and rinse them, then process them in a food processor, which will work better than a weak blender.

plant protein

the protein myth

If you've been a vegan for any amount of time, you have likely been asked, "But where do you get your protein?" Many people still think you need meat to survive or even be healthy. It seems so funny to me now, but those who are new and unfamiliar with this way of eating have understandable concerns. There is so much misinformation out there that vegans live off salads, are weak and frail, and don't get enough protein. It's completely false. There is so much protein in so many plant-based foods. I prove that with this book.

I've dedicated a lot of the recipes in this book to showing just how to get protein in your meals. I haven't been protein deficient since I went vegan in 2012 and have no problem building muscle either as a weightlifter or dancer. Making sure you are eating enough calories is so important and that, too, is easy to do with this book. I share many protein-forward mains for dinner and lunch, as well as filling breakfasts

and snacks (many also containing protein) that are healthy and contain hearty carbs and healthy fats. When you have all three of these macronutrients, you are getting a satisfying meal and enough calories.

The amount of calories needed will vary by person. These factors will be based on activity level, weight-loss or weight-gain goals, age, and gender. If you want a very specific customized idea of calorie needs, it is best determined by your doctor, a nutritionist, or a personal trainer. If you are looking for a more simplistic approach, you can use a calorie calculator found on numerous nutrition websites. Simply google "calorie calculator."

For example, I am forty-eight years old and weigh 138 pounds. If I wanted to maintain my exact weight at my current activity level, I would need 1,950 calories per day.

As a general rule of thumb, if I wanted to lose weight at my current activity level, I would need to decrease my calories by about 500 a day to lose an average of 1 pound per week.

In order to lose weight, you must burn more calories than you consume, creating a calorie deficit. Just be careful that if you don't want to lose muscle, it's important to be lifting weights and getting enough protein as well. Keep in mind that losing too much weight, too quickly, can result in muscle loss.

why we need more protein when we exercise

Let me break this down for you. Our muscles are made up of mostly protein. Therefore, for recovery, repair, and growth, it only makes sense that protein is required to "feed" our muscles. So, you definitely need to be mindful of your protein intake, not only to maintain the muscle mass that you already have but also for putting on more muscle and getting stronger.

Now, you may have heard within the plant-based community that "You don't need to worry about protein as long as you are getting enough calories." This is true if you lead a sedentary lifestyle, don't exercise, or don't have an interest in gaining muscle mass. You should get the adequate protein your body needs as long as you are eating enough. But since many people lead an active lifestyle and want to gain muscle, you will need more than the average person.

So, how much protein do you need?

Well, as mentioned above, if your goal is to gain muscle and you are lifting weights, a general rule of thumb recommended by the American College of Sports Medicine is to aim for 0.8 gram of protein per 1 pound of body weight. And there are many trainers that suggest 1 gram of protein per pound of body weight. So, if a person weighs 130 pounds, that would be a range of 104 to 130 grams of protein per day. I try to hit, personally, somewhere in the middle.

building muscle

I know not every person reading this book is worried about putting on muscle or even exercising, and that's totally fine! Many people are, though, and that's why this book focuses on protein-forward main dishes and lunches to help you get plenty of protein to facilitate muscle growth when coupled with weightlifting exercises. Protein focus is important if you're trying to put on muscle. When we weightlift, our muscles require protein for not only maintaining muscle, but also to repair and build more muscle.

Protein alone is not enough. You also need healthy carbohydrates and fats. They all play a role in a nutritious regime to build muscle. In this book, I show you how to put together fulfilling and nutritious meals containing each of these nutrients. We need a balance in order to look and feel our best. I share lots of protein-forward meals, along with filling side dishes and appetizers that contain healthy carbs, proteins, and fats, as well as vegetables for those amazing nutrients our body needs.

Individual goals and needs vary from person to person. It's important to consult your doctor or a nutritionist to determine this. If you are new to wanting to build muscle, the recipes in this book will help you do that, when combined with weight resistance training. You can hire a fitness coach or trainer if you are looking to start a program with weights to help get you on the right track.

amino acids
what are amino acids?

They are often referred to as the building blocks of proteins. They are molecules used by the body that combine to build proteins.

Our bodies need 20 different amino acids to function properly. Of these, 11 are called nonessential amino acids, meaning that our bodies make them on their own, regardless of the food we eat. The remaining 9 are called essential, which means we must obtain them from food.

- **The 11 nonessential amino acids are:** alanine, arginine, asparagine, aspartic acid, cysteine, glutamic acid, glutamine, glycine, proline, serine, and tyrosine.
- **The 9 essential amino acids are:** histidine, isoleucine, leucine, lysine, methionine, phenylalanine, threonine, tryptophan, and valine. Some foods contain all 9 essential amino acids, which are called complete proteins.

how to obtain essential amino acids

Since we now know that the 9 essential amino acids must be obtained through diet, let's go over how to do that.

- Animal products that contain all of the 9 essential amino acids are called complete proteins. Those are fish, chicken, beef, eggs, and dairy. Complete proteins are what we want to aim for in our diet each day, as much as possible. It is easier to get them on an animal-based diet since there are more foods that contain them.
- However, it is totally doable as a vegan. Plant-based foods that contain all 9 essential amino acids are soy products, quinoa, and buckwheat. Do not worry if you do not eat those foods. To form a complete protein on a plant-based diet, it is as simple as eating certain foods during the same day. An example of this would be beans with rice.

complete proteins

The plant-based foods that contain all 9 essential amino acids are as follows:

- Soy products including soybeans, tofu, soy milk, TVP, soy curls, tempeh, and edamame
- Quinoa
- Buckwheat
- Hemp seeds
- Chia seeds
- Lentils: These contain all 9, but they are low in the amino acid methionine, so it's best to eat them with a whole grain during the day to form a complete protein.
- Peas and pea protein (like in some protein powders): Like lentils, while peas contain all 9, they are also low in methionine and need to be paired with a whole grain to form a complete protein. Brown rice is a great choice.

Beans (with the exception of soybeans) do not contain all 9 essential amino acids, so they are not considered a complete protein. To make them a complete protein, eat them with a grain during the same day.

While it is important to have complete proteins in the food you eat each day, you don't need to worry about eating the lentils, beans, or chickpeas at the same meal as the grain. As long as you are consuming the amino acids during the day at some point, the body will absorb them from the foods you eat to form complete proteins. So, though it is pretty common to eat these together in the same meal, it's not an absolute must. The recipes in this book make all of these combinations easy to achieve on a plant-based diet. There are so many recipes that contain soy, chickpeas, lentils, and different beans, as well as plenty of grains, including quinoa. There is even a fabulous snack, my Seedy Coconut Trail Mix (page 201), that contains hemp seeds, which is a complete protein!

vegan protein sources

These are the protein sources that I prefer and use in this book, but some other options include soy curls, tempeh, and seitan.

tofu

Tofu is my favorite plant-based protein. There are endless ways to cook it and add incredible flavor and texture. It is high in protein, has a decent amount of fat, and contains all 9 essential amino acids! Since it has virtually no flavor on its own, it's a sponge to soak up the most amazing flavors from other ingredients.

Tofu is made from dried soybeans. The process involves soaking the beans in water, crushing them, and then boiling them. The mixture is then separated into solids and liquid. This liquid is soy milk, which will then turn into tofu when a coagulant is added to it. Tofu is so incredibly versatile. It is very filling, too. Tofu comes in different levels of firmness, including soft, silken, medium firm, firm, and extra-firm.

pressing tofu

Since tofu comes in packages with lots of water, it is important to drain and press the tofu before using it in a recipe, so the dish doesn't end up soggy and lacking flavor. If there's too much water in the tofu, it also won't brown as intended, or will be too bland. You can press it by placing the block of tofu onto a plate or cutting board with several sheets of paper towels on top. You will need to put something heavy on top of the paper towels like a few books so that the water will be pressed out. Alternatively, you can use a tofu press. Make sure to weigh the tofu after pressing, not before.

Some brands are more watery than others. I've found the only brand that is extra-firm and doesn't require any pressing is the Hodo brand.

legumes

Legumes represent most beans like pinto beans, black beans, navy beans, Great Northern beans, etc. Chickpeas (garbanzo beans), lentils, soybeans, peas, and peanuts are also all considered legumes.

lentils

Lentils are my second-favorite plant-based protein. They have a very mild flavor and absorb spices and marinades beautifully. There are different varieties: red, yellow, green, brown, and black. Since lentils are an excellent protein source, they are used many times in this book, in both sweet and savory recipes. The Chocolate Lentil Protein Muffins (page 45) use uncooked red lentils processed into a fine flour, for a protein source that is not protein powder. You can't tell the muffins have lentils in them either; they just taste like really rich and decadent chocolate muffins. The key is to really process them well into a fine flour. Lentils are also used in savory recipes like the Sweet Potato and Lentil Harissa Dip (page 50), Taco Lentil and Chickpea Lettuce Wraps (page 90), and the Pureed Red Lentil Curry Kale Soup (page 137). The lentils are all used in completely different flavor profiles and type of recipes, so each meal doesn't feel repetitive or similar.

chickpeas

Chickpeas are my third go-to for adding in protein to my diet. While they are higher in carbs than protein, they are still a wonderful ingredient to raise the protein content in plant-based meals. I love using them because they are so versatile and blend in easily to so many different types of dishes, absorbing the flavors really well. They also provide great texture, especially in the Caesar Smashed Chickpea Sandwiches (page 84). Additionally, they are a great choice for soups and curries to add a lovely, hearty texture.

protein powder

While not a whole food, protein powder is a good option if you are pressed for time or trying to get in extra protein. Some days, let's admit, can be crazy or busy and protein powder is quick, and can be thrown into smoothies, drinks, baked goods, and even oatmeal. While protein powder is not essential for meeting protein goals, it is a great choice for convenience.

There are so many varieties of protein powders on the market that it can be overwhelming choosing a brand. Many of them are loaded with artificial sweeteners or lots of questionable ingredients and additives. So, it's important to look for one that has quality ingredients and is made with fruits and vegetables and natural sweeteners. They also have many different types of proteins used in these powders: everything from rice, to peas, and even nuts or seeds.

I, personally, have used the Sprout Living brand for many, many years. They use high-quality fruits and veggies and no artificial sweeteners. They are sweetened with coconut sugar and a small amount of stevia. I use their Epic Protein Vanilla Lucuma and Epic Protein Chocolate Maca the most. They are absolutely delicious with no weird aftertaste and blend well into smoothies, as well as in baked goods. You can choose an unsweetened variety, though, if you prefer. If you choose to use this brand, use my code "thevegan8" and you can save 20% off all products.

Protein powder is a supplement, not a requirement for meeting protein needs or goals. You can absolutely obtain all your protein from whole foods if that is your preference.

protein powder in desserts

You can totally bake with protein powder. However, keep in mind that you shouldn't use too much. Protein powders can quickly go from being an addition to increase protein to overpowering the recipe. In other words, it can ruin a recipe if too much is used. And if it doesn't taste good in the end, what's the point?

I use protein powder in my Chocolate Protein Pancakes (page 29) for breakfast. The right amount is used because they just taste like delicious chocolate cake pancakes. They have no weird taste or texture. I've noted the appropriate amount of protein powder to use in each recipe.

how to build meals

To make sure you are getting adequate nutrition, with a balance of proteins, carbs, and fats, and your amino acids, you must learn how to properly build meals with these components:

- **Protein source:** Tofu, any soy products, lentils, beans, chickpeas. Keep in mind that beans and chickpeas all are higher in carbs than actual protein. They have good protein, but they are not as high in protein as vegan proteins like tofu, tempeh, and seitan.
- **Main starchy carbohydrate:** Grains like rice, quinoa, or pasta.
- **Nonstarchy carbohydrate:** Lower-calorie vegetables like all the green, red, orange, and yellow vegetables. This is where you would pick anything like spinach, broccoli, cauliflower, zucchini, or bell peppers of any color. Any of these will work. I personally love leafy greens like kale, spinach, collard greens, bok choy, or a salad combining several of these vegetables. These vegetables are low in calories, so you can eat a lot of them. They are high in fiber and antioxidants; both are important to overall health.
- **Fat:** Avocado, nuts, seeds, or the sauces in this book are great for a fat source at meals because many of them are nut-, seed-, or yogurt-based. Fats are important at each meal because they help to keep you full longer.

I've found the best way to get a balance, as well as satiety, is to pick a main food for the protein, like tofu or lentils. You can choose one of the mains in this book. If the recipe doesn't already have veggies and a carbohydrate like rice, grains, or potatoes, then you would choose one of those for your main carbohydrate. Next, you will select a vegetable, preferably a green variety. Last, add a small amount of fat to the meal, like a sauce or avocado. For the fat, it doesn't need to be much. Just so long as you have a little bit at each meal. Fat keeps us satiated because it is higher in calories. Even if you just use a drizzle of tahini, one of the many sauce recipes in this book, or some avocado, they will all work. Fats are also excellent for your brain health, as well as healthy skin, hair, and nails.

This way you will get a good overall balance of protein, carbohydrates, veggies, and a fat.

This is just meant to be a guide to help you build meals. Do not stress about perfection. You can do small amounts of different carbohydrates or switch the vegetables up. For example, some sweet potatoes and greens to go with a rice, as opposed to only rice or vice versa. Sometimes, I'll have a whole sweet potato with my protein and some greens. Other times, I'll have half a sweet potato and a little bit of a hearty grain. It really depends on what I'm craving. Just stick to getting a good variety of these foods each day and make sure you are sticking to a balance each meal and you will have a happy tummy and feel great!

first power meals of the day

Chocolate Chip Sheet Pan Pancakes _____ 27

Chocolate Protein Pancakes _____ 29

Curry Tofu Scramble _____ 33

My Go-To Protein Berry Smoothie _____ 34

Sweet Jalapeño Cornbread Waffles _____ 37

Peach Cream Cheese _____ 38

Pecan Pie Baked Oatmeal _____ 41

Apple Pie Overnight Oats _____ 42

Chocolate Lentil Protein Muffins _____ 45

Chocolate Chip Walnut Protein Bars _____ 46

chocolate chip
sheet pan pancakes

If you want to get your family and friends excited about pancakes, make these! They are so much quicker and easier than standing over a pan cooking pancakes one by one. For a more nutritious option, we are using white whole wheat flour. It is whole wheat (meaning it has the wheat bran and germ) but has a more neutral taste than regular whole wheat flour, which is too strong in flavor and quite dense. This is the perfect balance. The pancakes are fluffy and bursting with chocolate in each bite! As mentioned in Weighing Ingredients (page 14), I always recommend using a scale to follow my gram weights (no need to compare with cups) when working with recipes, especially flours, to get accurate results. The pancake batter itself is not very sweet at all, to accommodate for the chocolate chips and maple syrup that would be drizzled on top when serving.

2½ cups (280g) white whole wheat flour

¼ cup (40g) potato starch (see Notes)

2 teaspoons baking powder

1 teaspoon baking soda

½ teaspoon fine sea salt

1½ cups (360g) unsweetened almond milk (see Notes)

¼ cup (60g) unsweetened applesauce

5 tablespoons (100g) pure maple syrup, plus more (optional) for serving

2 teaspoons vanilla extract

4 teaspoons apple cider vinegar

½ cup (120g) dairy-free semisweet chocolate chips

Cut up fruit and other toppings (optional), for garnish

1. Position a rack in the center of the oven and preheat the oven to 375°F. Mist a 15 × 10-inch sheet pan well with cooking spray. Do not use a larger pan than this size or there won't be enough batter.

2. In a large bowl, whisk together the flour, potato starch, baking powder, baking soda, and salt. Add the milk, applesauce, maple syrup, vanilla, vinegar, and chocolate chips. Gently stir with a spoon just until moistened, being careful not to overmix, as overmixing can cause dense, tough pancakes. The batter will be lumpy and this is okay, they will bake up fluffy this way.

recipe continues »

3. Starting from the center of the sheet pan, pour the batter into the pan, spreading it into the corners with the back of a spoon, making sure it's even across. Pick up the pan and give it a little shake to even out the top.

4. Bake until a toothpick in the center comes out clean, 15 to 20 minutes.

5. Let cool for at least 5 minutes before slicing. Slice into squares and serve. Top with maple syrup (if desired), fruit, and any other toppings you like.

NOTES
- The potato starch replaces eggs to make these quite fluffy and not dense. It also adds a tenderness, keeping the whole wheat from making these too tough. Other starches will not yield the same results here, so it cannot be substituted. It can easily be found online on Amazon.
- I made these with almond milk with perfect results. I'm sure other milks will work as well, with the exception of soy milk. Since there is so much milk used, avoid soy milk, as it's very high in protein and would make these pancakes too tough and chewy.
- To make this recipe gluten-free, sub the white whole wheat flour and potato starch with 2¾ cups (340g) of King Arthur Gluten-Free Measure for Measure Flour. I found this brand gives the best results. All remaining ingredients are the same. This version takes closer to 20 minutes. Cool 15 minutes before eating to allow it to finish cooking, as gluten-free baked goods tend to be gummy if eaten too quickly.

NUTRITION: 348.1 CALORIES   6.6g PROTEIN   65.6g CARBS   8.3g FAT   7.9g FIBER   21.3g SUGAR   507.1mg SODIUM

chocolate protein pancakes

These pancakes are so delicious and will remind you of rich, chocolaty cake! And who wouldn't want cake for breakfast that is actually healthy, too?! I use the Sprout Living Epic Protein Chocolate Maca protein powder. Make sure you are not using toasted buckwheat, as the flavor will be overpowering. I purchase my buckwheat groats from Amazon, but some stores do carry them. If using store-bought buckwheat flour, it is important to use the beige light-colored buckwheat flour and **not** the gray-colored one. The gray is too strong in flavor. I find that it's very difficult to find the right color of buckwheat flour, so I just make my own in the blender (see Note).

¼ cup (40g) untoasted buckwheat flour

¼ cup (28g) superfine blanched almond flour

2 tablespoons (16g) cornstarch

1½ teaspoons baking powder

⅛ teaspoon fine sea salt

1 tablespoon (6g) unsweetened cocoa powder

3 tablespoons (27g) your favorite vegan chocolate protein powder

½ cup plus 2 tablespoons (150g) unsweetened almond milk, at room temperature (I use Malk, which is so creamy with no additives)

1½ tablespoons (30g) pure maple syrup or agave syrup, plus more (optional) for serving

½ teaspoon vanilla extract

Fresh fruit (optional), for garnish

1. In a large bowl, whisk together the buckwheat flour, almond flour, cornstarch, baking powder, salt, cocoa powder, and protein powder.

2. Add the milk, maple syrup, and vanilla and whisk gently until smooth. The batter will be thick and a bit gooey. (The gooey texture comes from the buckwheat flour, but do not worry, the cooked pancakes are not at all gooey.) Don't add more liquid, as that can add too much moisture and make the pancakes dense or undercooked in the middle.

3. Set the batter aside for 10 minutes. Letting the batter rest allows the baking powder and starch to absorb well, so you get fluffy results.

recipe continues »

4. While the batter rests, preheat a griddle or nonstick frying pan over medium-low heat, closer to low heat, so that the pan is nice and hot once the batter is ready.

5. I like to use an ice cream scoop for perfect size pancakes, but if you don't have one, use a ¼-cup measure to add batter to the griddle. Smooth out the tops if needed. Cook the first sides of the pancakes until the tops are looking dry all over and a few bubbles have formed, about 4 minutes. Don't flip them over too soon or the centers won't cook through. Flip and cook another 2 to 3 minutes on the second side or until done. Serve with fresh fruit and maple syrup, if desired.

NOTE I make my own buckwheat flour in my Vitamix. It only takes a few seconds and is much easier than trying to find the right kind of buckwheat flour. Add about 1 cup of unroasted buckwheat groats to the blender and blend, starting on low speed and increasing to high, for several seconds until completely fine. *Measure out only 40 grams for this recipe.*

NUTRITION (2 pancakes): 231.9 CALORIES   11.8g PROTEIN   32.2g CARBS   7.9g FAT   4.4g FIBER   8.6g SUGAR   524.6mg SODIUM

curry tofu scramble

This protein-packed breakfast is a fantastic start to the day and will give you so much energy and keep you full. I really wanted something more exciting than a basic tofu scramble for this book. I love, love curry, so that was the inspiration for this delicious, hearty breakfast that will become a staple. I love this with slices of fresh avocado and a toasted bagel.

14 ounces extra-firm tofu

6 tablespoons (90g) unsweetened almond milk or plant-based milk of choice

1 teaspoon yellow curry powder, homemade (see page 259) or store-bought

1 teaspoon garlic powder

1 teaspoon coconut sugar or ½ teaspoon granulated sugar

1 tablespoon (8g) nutritional yeast

½ teaspoon fine sea salt

¼ teaspoon freshly ground black pepper

½ cup (80g) finely chopped white onion

½ cup (75g) finely chopped red bell pepper

½ teaspoon packed minced fresh ginger

2 handfuls (40g) fresh spinach

TO PRESS TOFU   Use a tofu press if you have one. Otherwise, place several layers of paper towel on a large plate or cutting board. Set the tofu on the paper towels and top the tofu with more paper towels. Place a weight (like a skillet filled with canned goods) on top to help press the water out of the tofu.

1. Press the tofu (see left) and let sit for 15 minutes. You want the tofu dry, so it browns and absorbs the flavors well.

2. Meanwhile, in a small bowl, stir together the milk, curry powder, garlic powder, sugar, nutritional yeast, salt, and pepper until combined. Set aside.

3. In a large nonstick skillet, bring ½ cup (120g) water to a gentle simmer over medium heat. Add the onion and cook, stirring occasionally, until translucent, about 5 minutes.

4. Add the bell pepper and ginger and cook until tender, another couple of minutes. Add only a tiny amount of water, if needed, to prevent sticking.

5. Crumble the tofu and add to the pan, stirring occasionally, until the tofu starts to brown some, 3 to 5 minutes.

6. Add the reserved milk mixture and spinach, reduce the heat to medium-low. Stir to coat the tofu and spinach well, and cook for just a few minutes until warmed through and the milk is absorbed. Taste and add any additional salt or pepper, if desired.

7. Serve immediately.

NUTRITION: 129 CALORIES   11.8g PROTEIN   8.2g CARBS   5.6g FAT   2.8g FIBER   2.9g SUGAR   274.3mg SODIUM

my go-to protein berry smoothie

I really wanted to include this smoothie in the book since it has been my go-to for a few years now and so many of my followers love it. It makes a great breakfast if you are short on time, but I mainly use it as my post-workout smoothie! My go-to protein powder is by Sprout Living. It is sweetened. If you use a powder that isn't sweetened, your smoothie will be less sweet. I suggest thawing the fruit for 20 to 30 minutes before making the smoothie, as it helps the ingredients to blend easier and avoids the need to add extra water, which would dilute the flavors.

2 cups (280g) frozen strawberries

½ heaping cup (80g) frozen blueberries

3 tablespoons (30g) hemp seeds

⅓ cup (28g) frozen kale

1 tablespoon (15g) fresh lemon juice (omit if you prefer a sweeter smoothie)

¼ cup (25g) old-fashioned rolled oats (gluten-free if needed)

2 scoops (38g) your favorite vegan vanilla protein powder, preferably sweetened

In a blender, combine the strawberries, blueberries, hemp seeds, kale, lemon juice, oats, protein powder, and just enough water needed to blend and blend until smooth. Scrape down the sides as needed and do not add too much water or it will dilute the flavor. Serve immediately.

NUTRITION: 570 CALORIES   38g PROTEIN   48g CARBS   17g FAT   13.1g FIBER   22.9g SUGAR   291.7mg SODIUM

sweet jalapeño cornbread waffles

This may sound like an odd breakfast idea, but I love having unique breakfasts on occasion and wanted to break out of the expected flavors for a waffle. I was inspired to create a sweetened version of jalapeño cornbread, in waffle form! Oh my heavens, they are fabulous! You can choose the level of heat of your jalapeños (mild to hot) based on your personal preference.

1 cup (160g) yellow cornmeal

¾ cup (96g) superfine oat flour (gluten-free if needed)

3 tablespoons (24g) cornstarch or tapioca starch

2½ teaspoons baking powder

½ teaspoon fine sea salt

½ cup plus 2 tablespoons (150g) unsweetened almond milk

½ cup (120g) unsweetened applesauce

6 tablespoons (120g) pure maple syrup or agave syrup

¼ cup (35g) finely chopped pickled jalapeños, plus more (optional) for serving

¼ cup (43g) sweet corn kernels

Maple syrup and vegan butter (optional), for serving

1. In a large bowl, whisk together the cornmeal, oat flour, cornstarch, baking powder, and salt. Add the milk, applesauce, syrup, jalapeños, and corn and stir until evenly mixed and moist.

2. Preheat a waffle maker. I used the setting 4 on my waffle maker, but yours may vary. Once the waffle maker is ready, mist with cooking spray on the top and bottom waffle plates. Since the recipe is oil-free, my maker needed cooking spray so the waffles didn't stick.

3. Add about ½ cup of batter (again, depending on the size of your waffle maker, you may need more or less) and smooth it out. Make sure to leave about ½ inch gap from the batter to the edge to prevent spillage when closing the lid.

4. Close and cook according to the manufacturer's instructions. When ready, they should be golden brown and release nicely. Repeat with the remaining batter. Eat plain or top with maple syrup, vegan butter, and/or pickled jalapeños, if desired!

NUTRITION (1 waffle): 249.3 CALORIES   4.1g PROTEIN   54g CARBS   2g FAT   2.1g FIBER   14.8g SUGAR   449.4mg SODIUM

peach cream cheese

You don't need dairy to enjoy cream cheese! I've written many a cream cheese recipe over the years but they've all been made with different fruits and spices. This cream cheese is creamy, tangy, and so delicious. Serve on bagels or toast. Since we are using freeze-dried fruit, it is naturally sweet. Make sure you are using the freeze-dried fruit, which are dry and crunchy, NOT just dried fruit, which is chewy. Prep time does not include the hands-off soaking time. To make this a high-protein breakfast, I love to serve this cream cheese on a high-protein bagel. I love Dave's Killer Bread Epic Everything Bagels. This will make the breakfast 15g of protein per serving.

½ cup (70g) raw cashews, soaked (see Note)

56 grams (2 ounces) freeze-dried peaches

6 to 8 tablespoons unsweetened plant-based milk (the creamier, the better)

1 teaspoon apple cider vinegar

1 tablespoon (15g) fresh lemon juice

1 tablespoon (20g) pure maple syrup

⅛ teaspoon fine salt

Fresh sliced peaches (optional), for serving

1. Drain the cashews and rinse well. Add them to a food processor and process them into a fine crumble so they are no longer whole pieces.

2. Add the peaches, milk, vinegar, lemon juice, maple syrup, and salt to the food processor. Process for a minimum of 5 minutes, stopping to scrape down the sides a couple of times as needed. It will seem too gritty in the beginning, so process for several minutes and just be patient. It will eventually turn smooth and creamy.

3. Use immediately or place in the fridge to chill overnight to firm up. (I like it better cold.) Serve with fresh peach slices, if desired.

NOTE   Soak the cashews in a bowl of water for 8 hours minimum or overnight. This is not a step that can be rushed or skipped. If you do, you will end up with a gritty cream cheese.

NUTRITION (¼ cup): 121.1 CALORIES   2.7g PROTEIN   14.5g CARBS   6.8g FAT   1.4g FIBER   7.9g SUGAR   74.5mg SODIUM

pecan pie baked oatmeal

Get ready for a dreamy, impressive breakfast to serve to your family or guests. This pecan pie-inspired baked oatmeal not only tastes out of this world but smells amazing, too. I literally cannot stop making it for a weekend special breakfast. It reheats well and is filled with fiber and whole fats.

2 cups (200g) old-fashioned rolled oats (gluten-free if needed)

2 tablespoons (16g) ground flaxseeds (I use golden)

2 tablespoons (18g) coconut sugar or brown sugar

1 teaspoon ground cinnamon

½ teaspoon ground ginger

1¼ teaspoons baking powder

½ teaspoon fine sea salt

½ cup (67g) finely chopped pecan pieces, plus more (optional) for sprinkling

1¼ cups (300g) unsweetened plant-based milk (I used almond)

½ cup (120g) unsweetened applesauce

¼ cup (80g) pure maple syrup, plus more (optional) for serving

1 tablespoon (20g) regular molasses (not blackstrap)

1 teaspoon (5g) vanilla extract

Fresh fruit (optional), for serving

NOTE   To increase the protein content, use soy milk instead of almond.

1. Preheat the oven to 350°F. Lightly mist a 7 × 7-inch or 8 × 8-inch ceramic baking dish with spray, otherwise the oatmeal will stick.

2. In a large bowl, stir together the oats, ground flaxseeds, sugar, cinnamon, ginger, baking powder, and salt. Stir in the pecans.

3. Add the milk, applesauce, maple syrup, molasses, and vanilla and stir for a couple of minutes until everything is combined and the oats are completely wet.

4. Spread the mixture in the prepared dish and even out the top with the back of a spoon. If desired, sprinkle extra pecan pieces on top and lightly press them into the oatmeal mixture.

5. Bake until the oatmeal is firm around the edges and golden brown, about 35 minutes.

6. You can eat it right away, just spoon it into a bowl. I like to let it sit for at least 30 minutes to firm up (it'll still be warm) and cut it into firmer pieces. It tastes delicious on its own but is even yummier with fresh fruit and a drizzle of maple syrup right before serving. The baked oatmeal will last 3 to 5 days in the fridge and, of course, firm up much more. Reheat in the microwave or on low heat in the oven and serve.

NUTRITION (1 oatmeal square): 195.9 CALORIES   4.2g PROTEIN   28.5g CARBS   7.9g FAT   3.7g FIBER   11g SUGAR   202.8mg SODIUM

apple pie overnight oats

Apples are my favorite fruit, and pairing them with lots of warming spices and oats makes for a delicious, filling, and satisfying breakfast! Oats can be boring, but these amazing nutrition-packed oats are every bit as exciting as the start to your day should be! You can enjoy them cold after sitting overnight or briefly heat them in the microwave.

½ cup plus 2 tablespoons (150g) unsweetened almond milk or plant-based milk of choice (see Notes)

1 tablespoon (16g) nut butter (see Notes) of choice (with no added oils/sugar)

2 tablespoons (30g) unsweetened applesauce

½ to 1 tablespoon (10g to 20g) pure maple syrup or agave syrup

1 teaspoon coconut sugar

¼ teaspoon ground cinnamon

⅛ teaspoon ground allspice

⅛ teaspoon ground ginger

⅛ teaspoon ground nutmeg

Pinch of fine sea salt

¼ cup finely diced fresh apple (I used Honeycrisp)

½ cup (50g) old-fashioned rolled oats (gluten-free if needed)

1. In an 8-ounce mason jar or bowl with a lid, combine the milk, nut butter, applesauce, maple syrup, sugar, cinnamon, allspice, ginger, nutmeg, and salt and whisk well until smooth. You want to make sure the nut butter is mixed in. Add the apples and oats and stir well, making sure the oats are covered fully with the liquids.

2. Cover the jar or seal tightly and place in the fridge overnight. Enjoy the next morning.

NOTES
- Use sunflower seed butter to make this nut-free.
- To increase the protein content, use soy milk instead of almond milk.

NUTRITION: 380 CALORIES   11g PROTEIN   56.1g CARBS   14g FAT   7.8g FIBER   17.1g SUGAR   389.3mg SODIUM

chocolate lentil protein muffins

Who knew muffins packed with protein and lentils would taste so rich, chocolaty, and decadent?! Nobody will know that the main ingredient is lentils. These are a great sweet and healthy alternative to donuts for breakfast. I strongly urge you to weigh the ingredients, especially the red lentils, following my gram weights listed.

¾ cup (144g) dried red lentils

¼ cup (28g) superfine blanched almond flour

6 tablespoons (48g) tapioca starch

6 tablespoons (36g) unsweetened cocoa powder

1 teaspoon baking soda

½ teaspoon baking powder

½ teaspoon fine sea salt

½ cup plus 2 tablespoons (200g) pure maple syrup

½ cup (120g) unsweetened applesauce

1 teaspoon vanilla extract

¾ cup (180g) dairy-free semisweet chocolate chips

WARNING Do not overmix! If you taste the batter, you'll taste lentils, but don't worry, the end baked product is fabulous.

1. Preheat the oven to 375°F. Line 12 cups of a muffin tin with parchment paper liners.

2. In a high-powered blender or food processor, blend the red lentils until a superfine flour forms. The finer, the better, as this will affect the outcome of the muffin texture.

3. In a large bowl, combine the lentil flour, almond flour, tapioca starch, cocoa powder, baking soda, baking powder, and salt and whisk really well.

4. Add the maple syrup, applesauce, vanilla, and chocolate chips. Gently fold the ingredients together just until a moist batter forms.

5. Divide the batter among the 12 muffin cups. I like to use an ice cream scoop, as it gives the perfect amount to each liner and creates a dome top, resulting in better risen and fluffier muffins.

6. Bake until a toothpick inserted in the center of a muffin comes out clean, about 18 minutes.

7. Cool 15 minutes in the pan before eating, so they can firm up. Store in an airtight container at room temperature for up to 3 days.

NUTRITION (2 muffins): 408.8 CALORIES   10.1g PROTEIN   64.8g CARBS   13.6g FAT   8.4g FIBER   36.7g SUGAR   340.4mg SODIUM

chocolate chip walnut protein bars

These gluten-free protein bars are wonderfully hearty and loaded with good-for-you ingredients. They have lots of fiber from all the oats, and heart-healthy fats from the walnuts and flaxseeds. Protein powder gives these bars a boost of protein to start your day off right, and the crunchy walnuts add a buttery and exciting texture to the bars. I strongly urge you to weigh the ingredients, following my gram weights listed, as baking requires precision for the correct outcome. You don't need to compare the cups to the grams; just follow the gram weights.

1½ cups (192g) superfine oat flour (use gluten-free if needed)

3 tablespoons (24g) tapioca starch

¼ cup plus 2 tablespoons (48g) ground flaxseeds (I use golden)

¼ cup (36g) vanilla protein powder

½ cup (50g) old-fashioned rolled oats (gluten-free if needed)

2 tablespoons (24g) coconut sugar

2 teaspoons baking soda

1 teaspoon ground cinnamon

½ teaspoon fine sea salt

½ cup (160g) pure maple syrup

¾ cup (180g) unsweetened applesauce

½ cup (120g) dairy-free semisweet chocolate chips

½ cup (120g) finely chopped walnuts

NOTE If you want to skip the chocolate chips to reduce the fat and make the bars even healthier, you can omit them and sub in blueberries instead. To further reduce the fat content of these bars, simply reduce the quantity of walnuts by half to make them 9g of fat per bar.

1. Preheat the oven to 350°F. Lightly mist an 8 × 8-inch baking dish with cooking spray.

2. In a large bowl, whisk together the oat flour, tapioca starch, ground flaxseeds, protein powder, rolled oats, sugar, baking soda, cinnamon, and salt.

3. Add ½ cup (120g) water, the maple syrup, applesauce, chocolate chips, and walnuts. Gently stir until mixed, but don't overmix. Pour the batter into the prepared baking dish and spread out the top evenly.

4. Bake until a toothpick inserted in the center comes out clean with no batter on it, 25 to 30 minutes.

5. Let the bars cool in the pan and refrigerate for 1 hour. Since the bars are gluten-free, they need to be chilled before slicing, to ensure they don't fall apart. The chilling helps to set them and will make slicing much easier. After the bars are all sliced, they can be stored at room temperature or in the fridge, as desired.

CHOCOLATE CHIP WALNUT PROTEIN MUFFINS: You can also make these as muffins, if you prefer. Preheat the oven to 350°F. Line 12 cups of a muffin tin with parchment paper liners. Make the batter as directed and divide evenly into the muffin cups. They will fill up high. Bake until well risen, golden brown, firm to the touch, and a toothpick comes out with no wet batter, 20 to 25 minutes. (Mine were perfect at 22 minutes.) Cool 20 minutes before eating.

NUTRITION (1 bar or muffin): 288.1 CALORIES   8.1g PROTEIN   36.6g CARBS   13.5g FAT   4.2g FIBER   16.7g SUGAR   242.5mg SODIUM

impressive sides and appetizers

Sweet Potato and Lentil Harissa Dip _____ 50

Creamy Italian Dill Potato Salad _____ 53

Garlic Lemon French Green Beans and Tomatoes _____ 54

Miso Mashed Sweet Potatoes _____ 57

The Perfect Corn Salsa _____ 58

Garlicky Sun-Dried Tomato and Basil Rice _____ 61

BBQ-Spiced Sweet Potato Fries _____ 62

"Honey" Lime Miso Cauliflower _____ 65

Tim's Greek Salad with Homemade Feta _____ 66

White Bean Pinwheels _____ 68

Easy Go-To Flatbread _____ 71

sweet potato and lentil harissa dip

Ahhh, my beloved sweet potatoes! I love sweet potatoes more than any other food because of how versatile they are. You will see that I use them in both sweet and savory recipes in this book. I can turn a sweet potato into magic. Sweet potatoes go great with spiciness because the flavors can balance each other out. Harissa is quite spicy, so it works well here and gives an additional boost of flavor. This is a great dip to serve at parties. Serve with crackers and/or fresh veggies.

2 medium sweet potatoes (14 ounces/393g total), unpeeled

½ cup (100g) cooked green or brown lentils

3 tablespoons (45g) harissa (see Note)

2 tablespoons (30g) fresh lemon juice

2 large garlic cloves (5g), peeled but whole

¼ cup (60g) unsweetened creamy plant-based milk

½ teaspoon smoked paprika

¼ teaspoon freshly ground black pepper

NOTE This dip has a nice spicy kick due to the harissa brand I used (Sanniti). Different brands will vary and may be labeled mild to spicy, which can affect your result. I would suggest starting with 2 tablespoons first and tasting. Additionally, you may need a pinch of salt, for the same reason.

1. Cook the sweet potatoes (with skins on) either by baking or microwaving. They will be more flavorful this way, as opposed to steaming, which adds too much moisture to them. To microwave, cooking one potato at a time, wrap the potato with a paper towel and cook for 4 to 5 minutes until it is soft and squishy, so it will blend up beautifully (depending on the size of your sweet potato, the cooking time can vary). To bake in the oven, place the potatoes on a parchment-lined sheet pan and poke a few holes in each potato with a fork. Bake at 400°F until they are-fork tender and soft, about 45 minutes.

2. Peel the cooked sweet potatoes, slice them into chunks, and add them to a food processor. Add the lentils, harissa, lemon juice, garlic, milk, smoked paprika, and pepper. Blend for several minutes until very smooth and creamy. The longer you blend, the smoother it will be. If you want it less thick, add a touch more milk. It shouldn't need any salt since there is salt in the harissa. It should be sweet, creamy, a bit tangy, and have a nice kick of heat.

NUTRITION: 175 CALORIES   8.1g PROTEIN   35.3g CARBS   0.5g FAT   7.4g FIBER   4g SUGAR   235.9mg SODIUM

creamy italian dill potato salad

Potato salad is traditionally full of oil and eggs. I re-created this classic with the most delicious creamy dressing infused with an Italian flavor similar to a red wine vinaigrette. It's addicting!

2 pounds (910g) red potatoes

2 tablespoons (30g) red wine vinegar

1½ teaspoons fresh lemon juice

2 teaspoons salt-free Italian seasoning

½ cup (56g) raw hulled sunflower seeds

¼ teaspoon garlic powder

½ teaspoon fine sea salt, plus more to taste

Freshly ground black pepper

2 to 3 tablespoons (3g to 4g) chopped fresh dill, plus more for serving

5 tablespoons (20g) finely sliced green onions

1. In a large pot, combine the whole potatoes (with skins on) with water to cover by 2 inches. Bring to a boil and cook until they are fork-tender but still hold their shape, 15 to 20 minutes.

2. Meanwhile, to make the dressing, in a high-powered blender or food processor, combine ½ cup (120g) water, the vinegar, lemon juice, Italian seasoning, sunflower seeds, garlic powder, ¼ teaspoon of salt, and a few grinds of pepper. Blend until completely smooth and creamy, stopping to scrape the sides down as needed.

3. Drain the potatoes and cool completely. Once cool, cut them into about ¾-inch bite-size pieces. Transfer them to a large bowl. Add the remaining ¼ teaspoon of salt and more pepper to the potatoes before adding the dressing to enhance the overall flavor.

4. Pour the dressing over the potatoes, making sure to scrape out the blender well. Use two large spoons to toss the potatoes repeatedly until they are fully coated with the dressing. Add the dill and toss once more.

5. Cover the potatoes and refrigerate overnight to allow the flavors to meld.

6. Before serving, taste and add more salt and pepper, if needed. Add the green onions and more dill right before serving. It will last 3 to 4 days in the fridge.

NUTRITION: 157.1 CALORIES   4.9g PROTEIN   22.3g CARBS   6.2g FAT   3.2g FIBER   2g SUGAR   185.8mg SODIUM

garlic lemon french green beans and tomatoes

These green beans make an incredibly flavorful and quick side dish for dinner. They are light and refreshing and so easy to make. The juicy cherry tomatoes are a lovely contrast to the firm, hearty texture of the French green beans. The addition of garlic and lemon makes these two simple ingredients pop with flavor. Plus, I love that the green beans are so vibrant, making this side dish beautiful. The almonds add some healthy fat to the dish and a nice crunch. They are great served with the All-Purpose Smoky Tofu (page 277).

2 pounds (910g) French green beans

¼ teaspoon fine sea salt, plus more to taste

2 large garlic cloves, finely minced

10 ounces (283g) cherry tomatoes, halved

1 tablespoon (15g) fresh lemon juice

3 tablespoons (24g) sliced almonds

Freshly ground black pepper

1. In a large deep nonstick frying pan, bring 2 cups (460g) water to a simmer over medium heat. Add the green beans and salt and cook until they are crisp-tender and not mushy, 5 to 10 minutes.

2. Drain off any excess water and set the green beans aside in a dish.

3. In the same pan, heat a few tablespoons of water over medium heat. Add the garlic and cook, stirring often, until tender, 1 to 2 minutes.

4. Add the tomatoes and cook just until the tomatoes are slightly soft, only 1 to 2 minutes. They cook quickly and if you overcook them, they will fall apart and turn mushy. Remove from the heat.

5. Add the reserved green beans, lemon juice, and almonds to the pan. Toss to combine, making sure the green beans are well coated, evenly.

6. Season with more salt, if needed, and pepper to taste. Serve hot.

NUTRITION: 121.8 CALORIES   6.2g PROTEIN   20.8g CARBS   3.7g FAT   7.8g FIBER   9.7g SUGAR   138.6mg SODIUM

miso mashed sweet potatoes

If there is one food I could live off for the rest of my life, it would definitely be mashed potatoes and gravy. I typically have traditional mashed gold potatoes, but for this book I wanted something unique and unexpected, and these blew my mind with how creamy and satisfying they were . . . and the umami, salty bite of red miso was simply scrumptious! These are a great healthy carbohydrate side to a protein, like the All-Purpose Smoky Tofu (page 277) or the Almond Sesame Tofu (page 87) without rice.

2 pounds (910g) sweet potatoes, peeled and cut into 1-inch cubes

2 tablespoons (30g) red miso

½ teaspoon garlic powder

5 tablespoons (75g) creamy unsweetened plant-based milk (I used almond; see Note)

Fine sea salt and freshly ground black pepper

Fresh thyme leaves (optional), for garnish

1. Bring a large pot of water to a boil. Add the sweet potatoes, reduce the heat to medium, and simmer until they are fork-tender, 10 to 15 minutes.

2. Drain and add the potatoes to a large bowl. Add the miso, garlic powder, and milk. Use a masher to mash the potatoes to your desired consistency and until all of the ingredients are well mixed. I like mine extra smooth.

3. Season with salt and pepper to taste. Garnish with fresh thyme, if desired. Serve immediately.

NOTE   If you would like to make these potatoes higher protein, use soy milk.

NUTRITION: 175.5 CALORIES   4g PROTEIN   38.9g CARBS   0.8g FAT   5.9g FIBER   0.1g SUGAR   393.3mg SODIUM

the perfect corn salsa

Don't let the simplicity of this recipe fool you, this salsa is off-the-charts delicious! It truly goes with almost any dish as a wonderful topping or addition. The flavors are perfectly balanced. It is citrusy, sweet, a little spicy with a wonderful texture that will be a great addition to so many things like chili, tacos, burritos, but especially the Taco Lentil and Chickpea Lettuce Wraps (page 90)!

¾ cup (127g) frozen sweet corn kernels (not thawed)

½ cup (80g) finely chopped red bell pepper

¼ cup (40g) finely diced red onion

1 small fresh jalapeño (20g), seeded and finely diced

2 tablespoons (30g) fresh lime juice

2 tablespoons (6g) finely chopped fresh cilantro

¼ teaspoon fine sea salt

¼ teaspoon freshly ground black pepper

In a medium bowl, combine all the ingredients and stir well until everything is incorporated. Use immediately or chill in the fridge before serving.

NUTRITION (½ cup): 20.2 CALORIES   0.8g PROTEIN   4.5g CARBS   0.2g FAT   0.8g FIBER   1.9g SUGAR   124.6mg SODIUM

garlicky sun-dried tomato and basil rice

I love plain rice, but it's fun to eat something more elevated on occasion. This rice has a wonderful flavor from a subtle note of lemon and lots of garlicky flavor, with the delicious addition of sun-dried tomatoes and fresh basil. It is a great side dish to add to your meals. Serve alongside the Parmesan Ratatouille (page 118)!

1 cup (200g) white jasmine rice

1¾ cups (420g) low-sodium vegetable broth

4 large garlic cloves, minced (18g)

¼ cup (20g) dry-pack sun-dried tomatoes, finely chopped

1 tablespoon (15g) fresh lemon juice

¼ teaspoon fine sea salt

Handful of fresh basil (8g), finely chopped

1. Rinse the rice well, until the water runs clear, not cloudy.

2. In a medium pot, combine ¼ cup (60g) of the broth and the garlic and cook over medium heat, stirring often, until the garlic is tender, just a couple of minutes.

3. Add the rice, the remaining 1½ cups (360g) of broth, the sun-dried tomatoes, lemon juice, and salt and stir well. Bring to a boil. Reduce the heat to low, cover, and gently simmer until the rice has absorbed all the liquid, about 15 minutes.

4. Remove from the heat and let it sit for 5 minutes, covered. Fluff with a fork and stir in the fresh basil and serve.

NUTRITION (½ cup): 167.1 CALORIES   3.7g PROTEIN   36.8g CARBS   0.9g FAT   1.3g FIBER   3.3g SUGAR   130.2mg SODIUM

bbq-spiced sweet potato fries

Two things I love that are always at the top of my list are sweet potatoes and anything with barbecue flavor. So, joining the two was inevitable. I created my own barbecue seasoning that not only makes these sweet potatoes come alive, it can be used on any recipe you want to add a barbecue flare to. For even more barbecue flavor, you can serve these alongside my Texas BBQ Sauce (page 251) or the Healthy Ketchup (page 274).

2 medium sweet potatoes (1¼ pounds/570g total), peeled and cut into ¼-inch long strips

1½ tablespoons BBQ Seasoning (page 263)

1. Preheat the oven to 425°F. Line a sheet pan with parchment paper.

2. In a large bowl or zip-seal bag, combine the sweet potatoes and barbecue seasoning. Stir or shake to coat really well. You can use a light mist of cooking spray on the potatoes and toss if a more crispy result is desired. Spread out on the lined sheet pan.

3. Bake until fork-tender and no longer crunchy in the center, 25 to 30 minutes.

NUTRITION: 196.1 CALORIES   3.6g PROTEIN   45.9g CARBS   0.1g FAT   6.8g FIBER   9.5g SUGAR   367.3mg SODIUM

"honey" lime miso cauliflower

Cauliflower gets a bad rap and it's not that surprising because in its natural state, it tastes plain and, well, like nothing. But this sauce is tangy, sweet, with a salty bite from the miso and a little spicy from the pepper flakes. There is nothing boring about it at all. The tahini in this sauce provides a healthy fat, so it makes a great side dish to your main protein. It would be great to serve with All-Purpose Smoky Tofu (page 277) and some potatoes or rice as a grain to complete the meal.

2 pounds (910g) frozen cauliflower florets (no need to thaw)

3 tablespoons (45g) red miso paste

3 tablespoons (60g) agave syrup

2 tablespoons (32g) tahini (see Note, page 206)

1 tablespoon (15g) fresh lime juice

½ teaspoon garlic powder

¼ teaspoon ground ginger

¼ teaspoon red pepper flakes

1 teaspoon toasted sesame seeds

Chopped fresh parsley (optional), for garnish

1. Preheat the oven to 425°F. Line a large sheet pan with parchment paper.

2. Spread the cauliflower out on the pan. Bake until very golden brown, about 45 minutes. (Mine took this long from frozen.) Ovens vary, so watch that they don't burn.

3. In a small bowl, whisk together ¼ cup (60g) water, the miso, agave, tahini, lime juice, garlic powder, ginger, pepper flakes, and sesame seeds. If it is runnier than you'd like (depending on the brand of tahini), you can briefly heat it up over the stove to thicken the sauce.

4. Add the roasted cauliflower and sauce to a large bowl and mix to toss all the cauliflower until it is well coated. Serve immediately. If desired, garnish with chopped fresh parsley.

NUTRITION: 152.8 CALORIES   5.2g PROTEIN   22.8g CARBS   5.8g FAT   3.8g FIBER   13.1g SUGAR   461mg SODIUM

tim's greek salad with homemade feta

I had my mom taste-test this recipe for me and wow, she was over the moon! She raved about it and said it was better than any dairy and oil traditional Greek salad! She loved my homemade feta cheese and said it was better than the dairy version. While I have the feta in cubes in the photo for presentation, we both preferred it crumbled up to eat it, so there is a bit of feta in every bite. The original recipe comes from my amazing Greek dance instructor, Tim! He is a fabulous friend in my life and I wanted to honor him by sharing this recipe. I put my own twist on it to make it oil-free, and I also created a homemade vegan feta. Traditional Greek salad relies on a bit of olive oil. I write mostly oil-free recipes and took this as a challenge to make an incredible Greek salad, even without the oil. The homemade feta is the chef's kiss to this salad! Make it a day or two before you want to serve this salad, as the feta needs a night to marinate.

1 large cucumber (about 9 ounces/264g), halved lengthwise, then crosswise into half-moons

½ cup (80g) 2-inch long slices green bell pepper

1 cup (120g) cherry tomatoes, halved

½ cup (75g) 2-inch long slices red onion

½ cup (60g) kalamata olives, halved

1 tablespoon (15g) capers

2 tablespoons (30g) red wine vinegar

2 tablespoons (30g) low-sodium vegetable broth

2 teaspoons tahini (see Note, page 206)

¼ teaspoon garlic powder

¾ teaspoon dried oregano

Freshly ground black pepper

Fresh oregano leaves (optional), for garnish

½ cup Greek-Inspired Feta Cheese (page 271) or store-bought vegan feta

Fine sea salt (optional)

1. In a large bowl, combine the cucumber, bell pepper, cherry tomatoes, onion, olives, and capers. Set aside.

2. In a small bowl, combine the vinegar, broth, tahini, garlic powder, oregano, and pepper to taste and whisk very well until the tahini is mixed in.

3. Pour the dressing over the vegetables and gently toss everything so that the vegetables are well coated. The dressing will be thin and sit at the bottom of the bowl, but it will absorb into the vegetables as it chills.

4. Refrigerate the salad for several hours or overnight, gently stirring the dressing from the bottom of the bowl onto the vegetables again.

5. When ready to serve, you can leave the dressing in the bowl or drain it.

6. Top with fresh oregano, if desired, and pieces of feta cheese. Toss the salad once more and taste for salt and pepper, if needed.

NUTRITION: 134.9 CALORIES   5.3g PROTEIN   9.8g CARBS   8.6g FAT   3.3g FIBER   3.3g SUGAR   401.9mg SODIUM

white bean pinwheels

This perfect appetizer comes together easily and quickly. It packs so much flavor and is creamy thanks to white Great Northern beans. Most pinwheel recipes are made with chickpeas. I love chickpeas, but they are drier and less creamy than white beans, as well as stronger in flavor. These pinwheels have a great fresh taste and offer contrasting textures between the crispy red cabbage and creamy bean mixture. It's also a great appetizer for a party, and for that occasion I'd suggest doubling the ingredients for a larger portion for guests.

1 (15-ounce) can low-sodium Great Northern beans, drained and rinsed

1 tablespoon (15g) stone-ground mustard or Dijon mustard

1 tablespoon (15g) sriracha

1½ teaspoons fresh lemon juice

2 tablespoons (30g) tahini (see Note, page 206; or cashew butter if you don't like bitter tahini)

1 to 2 tablespoons (15g to 30g) vegetable broth

¾ teaspoon onion powder

½ teaspoon garlic powder

½ teaspoon fine sea salt, plus more to taste

¼ teaspoon freshly ground black pepper

1 large burrito-size flour tortilla

½ cup (30g) shredded red cabbage

Handful of fresh spinach (20g), roughly chopped

¼ cup (22g) packed sliced green onions

1. In a large bowl, mash the beans with a masher or fork until all the beans are no longer whole.

2. In a small bowl, combine the mustard, sriracha, lemon juice, tahini, 1 tablespoon of the broth, the onion powder, garlic powder, salt, and pepper and whisk well.

3. Pour this mixture over the beans. Mash repeatedly until thoroughly mixed and the mixture is creamy and smooth. It should basically be spreadable with the back of a spoon. If it's too sticky or stiff, add a second tablespoon of broth. Taste and add more salt, if needed. Depending on how salted the beans were, you may need some.

recipe continues »

4. Spread the bean mixture over the tortilla, leaving about ½ inch or so along the edge to prevent the filling from oozing out when rolling. Place the cabbage and spinach leaves on one side of the bean mixture and press it down flat. Add the green onions on top of the cabbage and spinach. Use your hands to tightly roll up the tortilla like a burrito. It will stick together once rolled up because of the sticky bean mixture. Squeeze it tightly and store either in the fridge for a couple of hours or about 1 hour in the freezer before slicing. It will be too soft to slice at room temperature.

5. Once chilled, use a serrated knife to trim off the uneven ends. Then carefully slice into 8 pinwheels, about 1 inch thick each.

NUTRITION (2 pinwheels): 178.2 CALORIES   8.3g PROTEIN   25.5g CARBS   5g FAT   5.7g FIBER   1.3g SUGAR   637.2mg SODIUM

easy go-to flatbread

These flatbreads will become a staple for your meals. This is the exact flatbread that I use to make personal-size pizzas every single week for my daughter and me. It is also the flatbread I use for the BBQ Jackfruit Cheese Pizzas (page 181), so I had to include it in this book since most commercial brands and recipes use oil. If you prefer to use these for dipping into curries or soups, then you will make them into 8 smaller sizes.

4¼ cups (510g) all-purpose flour, plus more for dusting

2 teaspoons baking powder

2 teaspoons garlic powder

1 teaspoon fine sea salt

1½ cups (360g) unsweetened canned "lite" coconut milk, at room temperature (see Note)

2 tablespoons (30g) unsweetened applesauce

1. In a large bowl, whisk together the flour, baking powder, garlic powder, and salt. Pour in the room temperature coconut milk and applesauce. Use a large spoon to stir the mixture together until it forms into a shaggy texture and no loose flour remains. Form roughly into a ball.

2. Flour a work surface and scrape the dough from the bowl onto the surface. Keep the flour handy, as you will need it to knead the dough. Adding flour, a little bit at a time, knead the dough for at least 7 minutes until it comes together into a smooth, pliable dough. You will need to add flour consistently, as it will be a bit too sticky without it. It helps to continue to add flour to the counter so it doesn't stick. To knead properly, you will continually rotate (turn), fold the dough in half toward you and press down with the heel of your hand and pushing it away. Do this repeatedly until it's stretchy and doesn't easily break when slightly pulling it.

3. Form the dough into a large smooth ball. If making large flatbreads (for a personal size pizza, 8 to 9 inches wide), divide the dough into 4 equal portions and roll into a ball. Using a bench scraper makes this easier. If you want smaller breads (for dipping into curries or soups, etc.), divide into 8 equal portions.

recipe continues »

4. Roll each piece into an oval shape between ⅛ and ¼ inch thick. It WILL poof up while cooking, so pay attention when rolling it that it's not too thick.

5. Heat a 10-inch skillet over medium-high heat. A cast-iron skillet will give the best results and beautiful browning. Once hot, lightly spray or brush with a tiny bit of oil if your skillet is not already well seasoned.

6. Add the first piece carefully and cook 2 to 3 minutes on the first side, or until golden brown underneath. A few bubbles may appear. Don't flip before it has browned.

7. Cook another 1 to 2 minutes on the second side. They will seem stiff when removing, but will soften perfectly within a couple of minutes.

NOTE   My recipe does not use oil, so the coconut milk is crucial to both the taste and texture. "Lite" coconut milk is very creamy and provides richness in place of oil, but does not leave a coconut taste (like high-fat coconut milk would). Low-fat milks will not work well at all and cause the bread to be dry and break easily. I recommend either the Sprouts Farmers Market brand or the 365 Whole Foods brand of lite coconut milk. Do not use the Polar brand; it is not made from pure coconut and will ruin the recipe.

NUTRITION (1 small flatbread): 135 CALORIES   4.8g PROTEIN   32.1g CARBS   2.5g FAT   1.9g FIBER   6.5g SUGAR   295mg SODIUM

fast and fabulous lunches

Pistachio Pesto Pasta _____ 77

Creamy Gochujang Chickpeas and Lentils
with Poblano Pepper _____ 78

Olivia's Pasta Alfredo with Fresh Basil _____ 81

Caesar Smashed Chickpea Sandwiches _____ 84

Almond Sesame Tofu and Rice _____ 87

Taco Lentil and Chickpea Lettuce Wraps _____ 90

Butternut Squash Curry _____ 93

Chickpea and Veggie Pita Pockets _____ 94

Lemony White Bean Basil Toasts _____ 97

pistachio pesto pasta

I am not exaggerating one bit when I say this is the most delicious pesto I've ever created or tasted. I was literally eating it straight from the blender. It is bold in flavor and has the most gorgeous bright green color. The pistachios add something special that pine nuts or other nuts do not. This pesto is different, richer, and has almost a buttery taste. It is incredible on pasta, as a pizza sauce, and as a spread on sandwiches. For the best results, I really recommend following my weights listed so the flavor turns out perfectly.

¼ cup (40g) raw pistachios

2 large handfuls of fresh spinach (30g)

1 large handful of fresh basil leaves (30g), plus more for garnish

1 tablespoon (15g) fresh lemon juice, plus more to taste

2 garlic cloves (8g), peeled but whole

1 tablespoon (8g) nutritional yeast or Lemon Parmesan Cheese (page 267)

½ teaspoon fine sea salt, plus more to taste

12 ounces pasta of choice (I used penne; see Note)

1. In a blender or food processor, combine the pistachios, spinach, basil, lemon juice, garlic, nutritional yeast, salt, and ½ cup (120g) water and blend until 100 percent smooth. You will need to scrape down the sides a couple of times during the process. It shouldn't be too thick, so it can easily pour over pasta. Taste and add more salt and/or lemon juice, if desired.

2. Bring a large pot of water to a boil, salt the pasta water well, add the pasta, and cook until al dente according to the package directions.

3. Add pasta to serving bowls and top with desired amount of sauce and toss. Garnish with fresh basil.

NOTE To make this higher protein, use a lentil or chickpea pasta in place of wheat and add All-Purpose Smoky Tofu (page 277).

NUTRITION: 392.7 CALORIES   15g PROTEIN   69.6g CARBS   6g FAT   4.6g FIBER   3.3g SUGAR   257.7mg SODIUM

creamy gochujang chickpeas and lentils with poblano pepper

This is easily one of my favorite recipes in the book. Not only is it very quick and easy, but it is high in protein from the chickpeas and lentils, while also being so rich in depth of flavor. It has a nice kick and is straight-up addictive! I've made this so many times since creating the recipe. If you've never tried gochujang (Korean chile paste), it is a worthy investment. It adds so much flavor and cannot be subbed. It is spicy, a little sweet, and really creamy. The tomato paste helps to balance out the spiciness of the gochujang by adding some acidity to the dish. To add a smoky element, I've included poblano peppers. All these bold flavors are magically softened by the creamy coconut milk.

1 large poblano pepper, diced (½ cup/70g)

¼ teaspoon fine sea salt, plus more to taste

3 large garlic cloves (12g), minced

2 tablespoons (30g) gochujang (Korean chile paste)

¼ cup (60g) tomato paste

1 (13.5-ounce) can unsweetened "lite" coconut milk (or another really creamy plant-based milk like unsweetened high-fat oat milk)

1½ teaspoons paprika

1 (15-ounce) can low-sodium chickpeas, drained and rinsed

1 (15-ounce) can low-sodium lentils, drained and rinsed

1 tablespoon (15g) fresh lemon juice

Cooked rice or other grain, for serving

¼ cup finely chopped fresh spinach or another green of choice, for garnish

1. In a large deep saucepan, combine ¼ cup (60g) water, the poblano pepper, and the salt and cook over medium heat, stirring occasionally, until the poblano begins to get tender, about 3 minutes.

2. Add the garlic and cook another minute. Add another splash of water if the pan is dry. Add the gochujang, tomato paste, coconut milk, and paprika and stir well until mixed thoroughly.

3. Add the chickpeas and lentils and mix well. Bring to a gentle simmer, then reduce the heat to low, cover, and cook until the

recipe continues »

sauce has slightly thickened and the chickpeas are tender, about 10 minutes. Remove from the heat and stir in the lemon juice. Taste and add more salt, if needed. (I added another ¼ teaspoon.)

4. Serve as is, or add rice or a grain of your choice to the serving bowls. Spoon servings of the gochujang sauce over the top. Garnish with the fresh greens.

NOTE This dish has a nice spicy kick. If you are really sensitive to heat, you can sub in green bell pepper for the poblano pepper and reduce the gochujang sauce to just 1 tablespoon. You may need to increase the salt then, as gochujang sauce has a lot of flavor in it. Make sure to use a creamy milk (like a high-fat creamy oat milk) and not a thin, watery one or the sauce will be less rich and flavorful. Avoid using full-fat coconut milk, though, as it is way too thick and will overpower the dish with coconut flavor.

NUTRITION (without rice): 316.8 **CALORIES**   16.3g **PROTEIN**   45.3g **CARBS**   8.8g **FAT**   14.4g **FIBER**   9.3g **SUGAR**   329.4mg **SODIUM**

olivia's pasta alfredo with fresh basil

I'm super excited to share this recipe with you because my daughter helped me to create it! If you've been a follower of mine for a while, you know that I have many Alfredo recipes to suit different tastes and allergies. My daughter has always loved my Alfredo recipes, especially my most popular garlic Alfredo on my blog. However, she and I both felt we could create an even better one. She helped me tweak the recipe using parts of my existing recipes to create BOTH of our favorite Alfredo sauce to date. She also suggested fresh basil to make it even better!

Fine sea salt

12 ounces pasta of choice, wheat or gluten-free (see Notes)

1 cup (240g) low-sodium vegetable broth

½ cup raw cashews (75g; see Notes) or sunflower seeds (56g)

3 tablespoons (45g) plain nondairy yogurt

½ cup (120g) mashed cooked gold potatoes (see Notes)

2 tablespoons (16g) nutritional yeast or Lemon Parmesan Cheese (page 267)

½ teaspoon onion powder

½ teaspoon salt-free Italian seasoning

2 large garlic cloves (8g), peeled but whole

1 teaspoon fresh lemon juice

½ cup fresh basil, roughly chopped, for garnish

1. Bring a large pot of water to a boil for the pasta. Salt the water well, add the pasta, and cook according to the package directions. Drain and set aside.

2. Meanwhile, in a high-powered blender, combine the broth, cashews, yogurt, mashed potato, nutritional yeast, onion powder, Italian seasoning, ½ teaspoon salt, the garlic, and lemon juice and blend until completely smooth. Taste and add more salt, if desired.

3. I feel the sauce is thick enough after blending and don't heat it. I just serve it directly with the hot pasta and it's perfect. However, if you want yours thicker, heat the sauce in a saucepan over medium-low heat, whisking constantly, until heated through and thickened to desired consistency, just a few minutes. Be careful not to cook too long or it'll get too thick.

recipe continues »

4. Add pasta to serving bowls and top with desired amount of sauce and toss. Garnish with fresh basil.

NOTES
- Use a chickpea or lentil pasta for higher protein content.
- If you do not have a high-powered blender (such as a Vitamix), you need to soak the cashews in a bowl of water to cover overnight. When ready to cook, drain and process in a food processor (which works better than a weak blender).
- Cook the potato using your preferred method. Boiling is not recommended, as it will dilute the flavor of the sauce. I just wrap a potato (with skin on) in a damp paper towel and microwave until soft. Remove the skin, mash, and measure out ½ cup (120g).

NUTRITION: 496.7 CALORIES   17.5g PROTEIN   82.7g CARBS   10.8g FAT   5.7g FIBER   5.3g SUGAR   302.2mg SODIUM

caesar smashed chickpea sandwiches

This is by far the most popular lunch recipe I've probably ever shared on my blog, so it was a must for the book. If you love Caesar salad, then you will love this magical sandwich! The recipe makes extra Caesar dressing so that you can spread it onto the bread for maximum flavor. I also love to use extra dressing for salads.

2 (15-ounce) cans low-sodium chickpeas, drained and rinsed

¾ cup (180g) Caesar Dressing (recipe follows), plus more to taste

½ teaspoon fine sea salt, plus more to taste

½ cup (120g) finely diced red onion

16 slices bread of choice

Optional toppings: any that you like (I used cherry tomatoes, lettuce, and hemp hearts/ sesame seeds)

1. In a large bowl, combine the chickpeas, dressing, and salt and mash until the dressing is evenly incorporated and the chickpeas are mashed but still have texture. Add the red onion and stir until mixed. Taste and add more salt, if desired. Depending on how salty (or not) your chickpeas were, it will affect how much salt you'll need.

2. Spread the chickpea mixture over half of the bread slices. (When assembling the sandwiches, I like to spread extra Caesar dressing on the bread like a "mayo" and as an extra boost of Caesar flavor.) Add any toppings you like and close the sandwiches.

NUTRITION: 278 CALORIES   18g PROTEIN   41.6g CARBS   7.5g FAT   7.2g FIBER   6.6g SUGAR   388.3mg SODIUM

recipe continues »

caesar dressing

Spread the dressing on sandwiches or use with salad greens.

¼ cup (60g) brine from a can of water-packed artichoke hearts

¼ cup (60g) fresh lemon juice

2 tablespoons (30g) Dijon mustard

1 cup raw cashews (140g; see Note) or ¾ cup sunflower seeds (112g)

½ teaspoon garlic powder

½ teaspoon freshly ground black pepper

¼ teaspoon fine sea salt, plus more to taste

NOTE If you do not have a high-powered blender (such as a Vitamix), you need to soak the cashews in a bowl of water to cover overnight. When ready to cook, drain and process in a food processor (which works better than a weak blender).

In a high-powered blender, combine the artichoke brine, lemon juice, ¼ cup (60g) water, the mustard, cashews, garlic powder, pepper, and salt and blend until completely smooth. It is a thick dressing, so you will have to scrape down the sides a couple of times to get it all to blend. Keep going until completely smooth. The dressing should be thick and creamy. Taste and add more salt, if desired.

Nutrition (2 tablespoons): 72 CALORIES, 2.1g PROTEIN, 4.6g CARBS, 5.6g FAT, 0.7g FIBER, 0.8g SUGAR, 85mg SODIUM

almond sesame tofu and rice

This dish is so easy and quick, yet really flavorful. The sesame oil is optional, but recommended because of the additional amazing flavor it adds. I love tofu for its high protein content and the fact that it's a complete protein. It is filling, and the healthy almond sauce boosts the healthy fat content. The combo of almond and sesame is so divine. To make this a hearty, complete meal, add greens of your choice. Steamed broccoli goes well here.

10-ounce block extra-firm tofu (see Notes)

¼ teaspoon fine sea salt

⅛ teaspoon freshly ground black pepper

1 teaspoon cornstarch

SAUCE

3 tablespoons (48g) creamy roasted almond butter (with no added oils/sugar)

2 tablespoons (30g) coconut aminos (see Notes)

1 teaspoon apple cider vinegar

½ teaspoon toasted sesame oil (optional)

½ teaspoon garlic powder

¼ teaspoon ground ginger

⅛ to ¼ teaspoon cayenne pepper, to taste

¼ teaspoon fine sea salt

1 teaspoon toasted sesame seeds

FOR SERVING

2 cups (240g) cooked rice

Sliced green onions

1. Press the tofu (see Notes) and let sit for at least 15 minutes. You want the tofu dry, so it browns and absorbs the flavors well.

2. Slice the tofu lengthwise into ¼- to ½-inch-thick pieces. You should have 22 pieces. Add to a bowl. Season the tofu with the salt and pepper. Sprinkle the cornstarch on the tofu and stir to evenly coat.

3. Heat a large quality nonstick pan over medium heat. (Using a nonstick pan, you will not need oil.) When the pan is hot, add the tofu in a single layer (not overlapping) and cook the tofu on the first side until golden brown, 3 to 5 minutes. Flip and brown the other side, about 1 minute. Remove the pan from the heat (but leave the tofu in the pan).

recipe continues »

4. Make the sauce: In a bowl, whisk together the almond butter, 3 tablespoons water, the coconut aminos, vinegar, sesame oil (if using), garlic powder, ground ginger, cayenne, and salt to taste (I added maybe ¼ teaspoon). The sauce should be runny.

5. Pour the sauce over the cooked tofu, return the pan to the stove, and heat over low heat just until warmed through and only slightly thickened. It will cook/thicken *very quickly,* so don't walk away. You don't want to overcook it or make it too thick. It should still be saucy. Sprinkle on the sesame seeds.

6. Serve hot over rice, with green onions.

NOTES
- I used a 10-ounce block of extra-firm tofu, but if you end up using 14 ounces, you may want to make 1½ times the amount of sauce, so there's plenty. Example: Instead of 3 tablespoons almond butter, it would be 4½ tablespoons.
- To press tofu: Use a tofu press if you have one. Otherwise, place several layers of paper towel on a large plate or cutting board. Set the tofu on the paper towels and top the tofu with more paper towels. Place a weight (like a skillet filled with canned goods) on top to help press the water out of the tofu.
- The coconut aminos add a touch of sweetness and are much less salty than soy sauce.

NUTRITION: 219.9 CALORIES   13.2g PROTEIN   9.8g CARBS   15.1g FAT   3.2g FIBER   3.4g SUGAR   502.3mg SODIUM

taco lentil and chickpea lettuce wraps

These wraps are smoky with a taco flavor and amazing texture and are the perfect complement to fresh, crisp lettuce. They are light, yet filling. They are good on their own, but become incredible when topped with my corn salsa, which is citrusy, sweet, and a little spicy. The combo is to die for!

TACO FILLING

1 (15-ounce) can low-sodium lentils, drained and rinsed, or 1½ cups (255g) cooked

1 (15-ounce) can low-sodium chickpeas, drained and rinsed, or 1½ cups (255g) cooked

2 tablespoons (30g) tomato paste

1 teaspoon chili powder

1 teaspoon ground cumin

1 teaspoon garlic powder

1 teaspoon onion powder

½ teaspoon dried oregano

½ teaspoon smoked paprika

¼ to ½ teaspoon chipotle chile powder

½ teaspoon fine sea salt, plus more to taste

¼ teaspoon freshly ground black pepper

WRAPS

6 butter lettuce leaves

½ cup The Perfect Corn Salsa (page 58; optional)

Sliced avocado (optional)

Sliced green onions, for garnish

1. Make the taco filling: In a large saucepan, combine the lentils, chickpeas, ½ cup (120g) water, the tomato paste, chili powder, cumin, garlic powder, onion powder, oregano, smoked paprika, chipotle powder, salt, and black pepper. Bring to a simmer over medium heat and cook until thickened and the chickpeas are soft, a couple of minutes. Taste and add more salt, if desired, which can depend on the salt level of the canned beans.

2. Assemble the wraps: Divide the mixture among the lettuce leaves and top with about 2 tablespoons of corn salsa, if desired. For an added fat, if desired, top with sliced avocado. Garnish with green onions.

NUTRITION (2 wraps): 263.3 CALORIES   16.5g PROTEIN   45.4g CARBS   3g FAT   14.6g FIBER   7.3g SUGAR   368.9mg SODIUM

butternut squash curry

This is the most delicious and easy curry that uses lots of healthy and wholesome ingredients! The butternut squash adds some sweetness to the spices from the curry and it's incredibly creamy. Using both my homemade curry powder and a red curry paste gives this curry maximum flavor. Pair the curry with rice for a complete protein and serve with lime wedges for squeezing and cashews, if desired.

2½ teaspoons yellow curry powder, homemade (see page 259) or store-bought

½ teaspoon garam masala

Fine sea salt

2 tablespoons (30g) vegan Thai red curry paste

2 tablespoons (30g) coconut aminos

½ cup (120g) plain tomato sauce/passata

1 cup (160g) finely diced red onion

1 (13.6-ounce) can unsweetened "lite" coconut milk

4 cups (480g) ¾- to 1-inch chunks peeled butternut squash

1 (15-ounce) can low-sodium chickpeas, drained and rinsed, or 1½ cups (255g) cooked chickpeas

4 large handfuls of fresh spinach leaves (90g)

Cooked rice or grain of choice (optional), for serving

1. In a bowl, stir together the curry powder, garam masala, ¼ teaspoon salt, the curry paste, coconut aminos, and tomato sauce until well combined.

2. In a large deep saucepan, combine the red onion, a pinch of salt, and ¼ cup (60g) water and bring to a simmer over medium heat. Simmer, stirring occasionally, until the onion caramelizes and starts to turn brown, about 10 minutes. Add tiny amounts of water only as needed to prevent burning.

3. Add the curry paste/spice mixture to the pan and stir for 30 seconds to release their aromas. Add the coconut milk, ¼ cup (60g) water, and the butternut squash. Stir until fully mixed. Bring to a simmer, cover, and cook until the butternut squash is tender, about 10 minutes.

4. Add the chickpeas, reduce the heat to medium-low, cover, and cook until the squash is fork-tender and the curry has thickened and become creamy and saucy, 5 to 10 minutes.

5. Stir in the spinach and heat through just until wilted.

6. Serve as is or with cooked grain of choice.

NUTRITION: 238 CALORIES   8.6g PROTEIN   33.7g CARBS   9g FAT   8.5g FIBER   8.5g SUGAR   724.1mg SODIUM

chickpea and veggie pita pockets

These chickpeas have the most delicious flavor, despite their simplicity, and you will want to make them on the regular. Pairing them with fresh spinach, bell peppers, and my lemon herb tahini sauce packs so much nutrition and flavor. I find that fresh spinach, not cooked, adds the best texture here. These make a delicious, healthy lunch full of protein and healthy carbs. The herby dressing is a great tangy contrast to the slightly sweet, smoky chickpeas, and also provides moisture to the pitas.

2 (15-ounce) cans low-sodium chickpeas, drained and rinsed, or 3 cups cooked (510g)

1 large red bell pepper (5½ ounces/160g), thinly sliced

1 tablespoon (15g) minced garlic

3 tablespoons (45g) coconut aminos

2 tablespoons (30g) sriracha

1 teaspoon liquid smoke

1 large handful of fresh spinach (30g), roughly chopped

2 (7-inch) whole wheat pitas with pockets

Lemon Herb Tahini Sauce (page 243), for serving

NOTES

- A quality nonstick pan should prevent sticking, but if necessary, use a little cooking spray.
- If eating for one, prepare just one pita pocket to eat and not all of them, so they don't get soggy from the dressing.

1. In a large quality nonstick skillet (see Notes), cook the chickpeas over medium-high heat, stirring often, until golden brown, about 10 minutes. Add the bell pepper and cook until the peppers are tender, 3 to 5 minutes.

2. Add the garlic, coconut aminos, sriracha, and liquid smoke and stir very well until the chickpeas are well coated. Cook for only 1 to 2 minutes to heat the liquids and cook the garlic. Remove the chickpea mixture from the heat and stir in the spinach.

3. Slightly warm the pita pockets for a few seconds in the microwave. Slice them in half. Add about ¾ cup or so of the chickpea mixture to each half of the pita pocket. Spoon 1 to 2 tablespoons (or as much as desired) of the lemon herb tahini sauce to each pita pocket and serve immediately.

NUTRITION (1 whole pita): 576.4 CALORIES   27.8g PROTEIN   105g CARBS   7.6g FAT   23.7g FIBER   22.9g SUGAR   1216.4mg SODIUM

lemony white bean basil toasts

This recipe may look really simple, and it is, but oh boy did I fall in love with how delicious it is! It's lemony, creamy, filling, and so delicious on toast. I love basil so much and blending it with creamy white beans and bright lemon made for one yummy lunch. It is satiating, yet also light. The carbs from the beans and bread will keep your tummy happy and full. When processing, I left little pieces of basil because I liked the look and surprise pop of basil texture in my mouth, as opposed to completely blending them.

1 (15-ounce) can low-sodium white beans (Great Northern or cannellini), drained and rinsed, or 1½ cups (255g) cooked beans

2 tablespoons (30g) low-sodium vegetable broth

2 tablespoons (30g) fresh lemon juice

1 teaspoon garlic powder

1 teaspoon onion powder

½ teaspoon fine sea salt, plus more to taste

Freshly ground black pepper

Handful of fresh basil leaves (11g) plus more (optional) for garnish

3 slices bread of choice, toasted

1. In a food processor, combine the beans, broth, lemon juice, garlic powder, onion powder, salt, and a few grinds of pepper and process until completely smooth and creamy. Add the basil and process either fully or leaving little tiny pieces throughout. Taste and add more salt if needed (this will depend on the saltiness of the beans you use).

2. Serve on toast (garnished with basil, if desired) for a wonderful, feel-good lunch!

NOTE This is a high-protein, high-carb, and low-fat lunch. If you would like to add more fat, add sliced avocado on top of the toasts or add 1 tablespoon tahini to the white bean puree when blending.

NUTRITION: 189.7 CALORIES   11g PROTEIN   34.5g CARBS   1.4g FAT   6.6g FIBER   2.1g SUGAR   434.9mg SODIUM

casseroles you'll crave

Teriyaki Orzo Casserole _____ 100

Vegan "Tuna" Casserole _____ 103

Pecan Stuffing _____ 105

Hungarian Sült Polenta Margherita _____ 109

Skillet Chickpea Quinoa Casserole _____ 111

Cheesy Lentil Pasta Bake _____ 114

Baked Pumpkin Sage Risotto _____ 117

Parmesan Ratatouille _____ 118

teriyaki orzo casserole

This casserole is packed with protein, as well as veggies and flavor! I'm a huge lover of teriyaki sauce, so this casserole was inspired by that. It is also very easy and quick to make. I love all the texture in every bite. This whole dish is so addicting, but also one you can feel good about eating. It's also so gorgeous, bright, and colorful, and sure to be a showstopper!

¾ cup (180g) teriyaki sauce, homemade (see page 248) or store-bought

12 ounces extra-firm tofu

1 cup (168g) orzo pasta

4 cups (9 ounces/255g) chopped broccoli florets, steamed or slightly precooked

1 (8-ounce) bag fresh sugar snap peas

1 cup (150g) frozen shelled edamame, precooked (see Notes)

¾ cup (85g) shredded carrots

½ teaspoon ground ginger

¼ teaspoon freshly ground black pepper

2 tablespoons (20g) toasted sesame seeds

¼ cup sliced green onions, for garnish

1. If making homemade teriyaki sauce, it's best made the day before, as it thickens to the perfect consistency overnight.

2. Slice the tofu into bite-size pieces, about 1 inch thick, and press (see Notes) for 15 minutes. This is very important so it is not soggy or bland in the casserole.

3. In a saucepan, bring 2 cups (480g) water to a boil. Add the orzo, immediately reduce the heat to low, cover, and simmer until tender, about 10 minutes. Drain any excess water.

4. Preheat the oven to 375°F. Lightly mist a 9 × 13-inch baking dish with cooking spray.

5. In a large bowl, combine the cooked orzo, broccoli, sugar snap peas, edamame, carrots, ginger, and pepper and gently toss. Add the teriyaki sauce and the tofu and gently toss once more until everything is coated evenly with the teriyaki sauce. Pour the mixture into the prepared baking dish.

6. Bake for 15 minutes, uncovered, until hot. Garnish with sesame seeds and green onions before serving.

NUTRITION: 251 CALORIES   16g PROTEIN   31.5g CARBS   7.5g FAT   7.9g FIBER   9.2g SUGAR   1201.8mg SODIUM

NOTES

- To make this soy-free, replace the teriyaki sauce with the soy-free version on my website or in my first cookbook. Omit the tofu and replace the edamame with green peas or cooked chickpeas for higher protein options.

- To press tofu: Use a tofu press if you have one. Otherwise, place several layers of paper towel in a large bowl. Set the tofu on the paper towels and top with more paper towels. Place a weight (like a skillet filled with canned goods) on top to help press the water out of the tofu.

- For gluten-free, use a gluten-free orzo or 2 cups cooked brown rice.

- To precook the edamame, microwave for 3 to 4 minutes. It should be almost fully tender and will finish cooking in the oven to the perfect tender yet firm texture.

vegan "tuna" casserole

I loved my mom's tuna casserole growing up. In fact, I was obsessed with it, and I've missed it ever since going vegan. So, I finally created a vegan version! Now, of course it doesn't taste identical since we aren't using actual tuna, but it does have a seafood flavor and a rich, flavorful creamy sauce like the dairy version. I used regular wheat noodles because I wanted that classic taste as much as possible and didn't care for the lentil noodles in my trials, but lentil noodles will work if you're looking for gluten-free.

Fine sea salt

3 cups (225g) rotini or fusilli pasta

1 (14-ounce) can hearts of palm, drained

¾ cup raw cashews (115g; see Notes) or sunflower seeds (84g)

4 tablespoons (32g) nutritional yeast

4 sheets nori

1½ tablespoons (23g) Dijon mustard

2 teaspoons fresh lemon juice

1 teaspoon garlic powder

1½ teaspoons onion powder

¼ teaspoon celery seeds

¼ teaspoon freshly ground black pepper, plus more to taste

⅛ teaspoon cayenne pepper

1 cup (150g) green peas

½ cup (50g) shredded carrots, slightly precooked (see Notes)

¼ cup (20g) panko bread crumbs (optional) or Lemon Parmesan Cheese (page 267)

2 tablespoons chopped fresh parsley (optional), for garnish

1. Bring a pot of water to a boil for the pasta. Salt the water well, add the pasta, and cook according to the package directions. Drain and set aside.

2. Preheat the oven to 375°F. Lightly mist a 9 × 13-inch baking dish with cooking spray.

3. In a food processor, briefly process the drained hearts of palm into small pieces that resemble tuna. Set aside.

4. In a high-powered blender, combine 1½ cups (360g) water, the cashews, nutritional yeast, nori sheets, mustard, lemon juice, garlic powder, onion powder, celery seeds, 1 teaspoon salt, the black pepper, and cayenne and blend until completely creamy and no bits of nuts remain. Taste the sauce. It should be very rich and have a noticeable seafood flavor. It needs to be strong so that the finished casserole is flavorful when mixed in with the pasta.

recipe continues »

5. Add the cooked pasta, processed hearts of palm, blended sauce, peas, carrots, and panko crumbs, if desired, to the baking dish and toss everything together carefully until fully mixed. Taste and add more salt and pepper, if needed.

6. Bake about 20 minutes, until bubbling hot.

7. Top with the fresh parsley, if desired, and serve immediately.

NOTES

- If you do not have a high-powered blender (such as a Vitamix), you need to soak the cashews in a bowl of water to cover overnight. When ready to cook, drain and process in a food processor (which works better than a weak blender).
- Precook your carrots by putting them in the microwave for 2 minutes. Precooking will soften them and make them less crunchy in the dish.
- For a higher protein option, swap the wheat noodles for lentil pasta and replace the green peas with cooked shelled edamame. Please keep in mind it will change the classic taste with these options.

NUTRITION: 393.7 CALORIES   15.5g PROTEIN   61.4g CARBS   10.2g FAT   6g FIBER   15.4g SUGAR   419.1mg SODIUM

pecan stuffing

This stuffing is like no other you've probably ever had. It has no oil or butter in it, but you'd never know it. I used finely chopped pecans here for a delicious, deep buttery flavor to replace any oil. The fresh herbs take it to the next level and the whole dish will make all your guests huge fans. It is great any time of the year, but of course, especially Thanksgiving.

1-pound (455g) loaf ciabatta bread, cut into 1-inch cubes

1 cup (160g) roughly chopped red onion

1 cup (115g) chopped celery (3 to 4 stalks)

5 large garlic cloves (15g), minced

¾ teaspoon fine sea salt

3 tablespoons (8g) minced fresh herbs (see Notes)

2 cups (480g) low-sodium vegetable broth

2 teaspoons (10g) vegan Worcestershire sauce

¾ cup (90g) finely chopped pecans

¼ teaspoon freshly ground black pepper

1. Place the cubed bread on a sheet pan and set out at room temperature for at least 8 hours or overnight. This will dry out the bread well so it holds its texture for the stuffing. Don't skip this step or you will end up with soggy stuffing.

2. Preheat the oven to 350°F. Mist a 4-quart baking dish or two 8 × 8-inch baking dishes with cooking spray. (It's important to spray your dish or the stuffing will stick badly.)

3. Spread the bread in the baking dish(es).

4. In a large pan, combine the onion, celery, garlic, ¼ teaspoon of the salt, and 6 tablespoons (90g) water. Bring to a simmer over medium heat and cook, stirring often, until tender and ALL the water is gone, 5 to 8 minutes. Add the fresh herbs and stir constantly for about 30 seconds until fragrant. Remove the veggie/herb mixture from the heat.

5. In a large bowl, combine the veggie/herb mixture, broth, Worcestershire sauce, pecans, remaining ½ teaspoon of salt, and the black pepper. Pour this mixture over the bread in the baking dish(es) and toss well for 3 to 5 minutes until all the bread is coated and moist. It will seem too dry at first, but keep stirring

recipe continues »

until the liquid is no longer sitting at the bottom to ensure it bakes correctly.

6. Cover with foil and bake for 30 minutes.

7. Remove the foil and bake until the top is golden brown and the tips of the bread are crispy, another 25 minutes.

8. Cool for 5 minutes and then serve.

NOTES

- You can use another type of bread that is similar in texture to a ciabatta, like a sourdough or French loaf. You want a sturdy loaf, so it holds up well and doesn't get soggy.
- For the herbs, I used 2 tablespoons sage and 1 tablespoon thyme. Definitely don't omit the sage since it's a classic flavor in stuffing! I also like to add extra minced fresh sage and thyme for serving, but this is optional.

NUTRITION: 333.5 CALORIES   9.6g PROTEIN   48g CARBS   12g FAT   5.8g FIBER   5.4g SUGAR   649.8mg SODIUM

hungarian sült polenta margherita

This recipe was inspired by my incredible Hungarian dance teacher, Richie! The original recipe he gave me is made with dairy-based pesto and dairy mozzarella cheese, so I adapted the recipe quite a bit from the original to make it vegan and oil-free. I used instant polenta to save time, and you can always use a store-bought vegan parmesan and mozzarella cheese for added convenience. But I think it's extra amazing when you use the homemade vegan cheeses from this book! I used parmesan cheese in the polenta (instead of pesto and mozzarella) so it would firm up. It turned out amazing and is a truly unique way to eat polenta: Think classic margherita pizza, but with baked (sült) polenta as the base instead of pizza crust!

4 cups (960g) low-sodium vegetable broth

1 cup (160g) instant polenta

¾ teaspoon fine sea salt, plus more to taste

½ cup (60g) Lemon Parmesan Cheese (page 267) or store-bought vegan parmesan

1 teaspoon garlic powder

Small handful of fresh basil leaves (10g), roughly chopped, plus 9 leaves for topping

Freshly ground black pepper

1 cup (240g) canned crushed fire-roasted tomatoes

½ cup (120g) vegan mozzarella, homemade (see page 268) or store-bought, preferably a liquid/soft version and not shredded

1. Preheat the oven to 400°F. Lightly mist an 8 × 8-inch baking dish with cooking spray.

2. In a large pot, bring the broth to a rapid boil over high heat. Once boiling, remove from the heat and add the polenta slowly and whisk in for a couple of minutes until it becomes very thick. Immediately add the salt, parmesan, garlic powder, and chopped basil and stir well. Taste and season with pepper and more salt, if needed.

3. Add the polenta mixture to the baking dish and spread out evenly and smooth out the top.

4. Bake until it firms up and is a bit golden along the edges, about 30 minutes.

recipe continues »

5. Spread the tomatoes over the top. Place the 9 basil leaves on top and then add large spoonfuls of the mozzarella cheese on top. Smooth out the cheese a bit if it's thick from the fridge.

6. Return to the oven and bake until the cheese is melted and golden, 25 to 30 minutes.

7. Let the polenta cool about 10 minutes or so to firm up more before serving. It should be a lot firmer by this point.

NOTE If you will be making my parmesan cheese and mozzarella recipes, I highly suggest making them the day before to save time. That way, when you are ready to make this recipe, it's much easier to just add them to the cooked polenta and bake.

NUTRITION: 271.8 CALORIES   9.1g PROTEIN   46.4g CARBS   5.5g FAT   3.7g FIBER   6.2g SUGAR   626.6mg SODIUM

skillet chickpea quinoa casserole

After I made this, I didn't even bother putting it on a plate, I just kept eating it straight from the skillet. It is that good! Quinoa is a wonderful ingredient in a plant-based diet because it is a complete protein, containing all nine essential amino acids. This recipe is packed with nutrition from the quinoa, additional protein from the chickpeas, and fiber and antioxidants from the spinach. It has a mild spicy flavor and warming taste from the spices. It is also one of the easiest and fastest casseroles you'll ever make. The casserole itself is filling and satisfying and I loved it as is, but if you would like a richer, more indulgent version, add the optional cheese on top or even sliced avocado for another great healthy fat option!

1 cup (188g) white quinoa, rinsed well

¾ teaspoon fine sea salt, plus more to taste

1 (15-ounce) can crushed fire-roasted tomatoes

1½ teaspoons chili powder

1½ teaspoons garlic powder

¼ teaspoon ground cumin

1½ teaspoons onion powder

1 teaspoon salt-free Italian seasoning

¼ teaspoon red pepper flakes

¼ teaspoon freshly ground black pepper

¼ heaping cup (40g) kalamata olives, finely diced

2 large handfuls of fresh spinach (40g), roughly chopped

½ cup vegan mozzarella (optional), homemade (see page 268) or store-bought

Sliced avocado (optional)

1. In a medium pot, combine the quinoa, 2 cups (480g) water, and ¼ teaspoon of the salt and stir well. Bring to a boil. Reduce the heat to low, cover, and simmer for 15 minutes. Remove from the heat and let sit covered for 5 minutes and then fluff the quinoa with a fork.

2. Preheat the oven to 375°F.

3. In a medium bowl, combine the tomatoes, chili powder, garlic powder, cumin, onion powder, Italian seasoning, pepper flakes, remaining ½ teaspoon of salt, and the pepper and stir well.

4. Add the olives, spinach, and cooked quinoa to the bowl of tomatoes and spices and stir well until all the quinoa is evenly coated. Taste and add more salt, if needed.

recipe continues »

5. Add this mixture to a 10-inch cast-iron skillet and spread out the top. Bake for 15 to 20 minutes until hot. If using a homemade or store-bought (solid or shredded) mozzarella, remove the skillet from the oven, top with the cheese, and bake for another 5 minutes or so until the cheese is firm (if using mine) or melted (if using store-bought). If using a store-bought liquid mozzarella, like the Miyoko's brand, add it to the skillet before baking and then bake for 15 to 20 minutes, as it will need that long to firm up.

6. Serve hot, with sliced avocado if you didn't choose the cheese topping.

NUTRITION: 241.8 CALORIES   8.3g PROTEIN   38.7g CARBS   6.1g FAT   6.6g FIBER   2.8g SUGAR   798.3mg SODIUM

cheesy lentil pasta bake

Cheesy, protein-packed, comforting, and delicious! What more could you want? This dish is so filling because it's loaded with plant-based protein and healthy fats. For the sauce, you can use either my five-minute pizza sauce, a store-bought variety, or even a marinara. This dish also reheats really well for lunch the next day. Just a tip, kids may be more sensitive to the texture of lentil pasta, so use regular pasta if that's an issue. My daughter prefers wheat pasta in this recipe.

1 cup (240g) liquid vegan mozzarella, homemade (see page 268) or store-bought

Fine sea salt

8 ounces lentil pasta or pasta of choice

2 cups (480g) pizza sauce, homemade (see page 252) or store-bought

3 tablespoons (48g) tahini (see Note, page 206)

2 tablespoons (16g) nutritional yeast

1 (15-ounce) can lentils, drained and rinsed

½ cup (62g) sliced black olives

2 large handfuls of fresh spinach (40g)

½ teaspoon red pepper flakes, plus more (optional) to taste

Fresh basil, for garnish

NOTE To save time, make the homemade mozzarella and pizza sauce the day before so this meal comes together quickly. The mozzarella will thicken and firm up in the fridge, so I recommend blending it before using to bring it back to a liquid state so that it's easy to mix in the dish before baking.

1. If using my homemade mozzarella, make that before beginning the recipe.

2. Bring a pot of water to a boil for the pasta. Salt the water well, add the pasta, and cook according to the package directions. Drain and set aside.

3. Preheat the oven to 400°F.

4. In a large bowl, stir together the pizza sauce, tahini, and nutritional yeast.

5. Add the cooked pasta to an 8 × 8-inch baking dish and stir in the pizza sauce mixture. Add the lentils, olives, spinach, and pepper flakes and stir until well combined and all the pasta is coated. Taste and add salt, if needed (this can vary based on the sauce used).

6. Stir ½ cup (120g if using homemade) of the mozzarella into the pasta and mix evenly. Top with the remaining cheese and spread out evenly with the back of a spoon. Top with extra red pepper flakes, if desired.

7. Bake, uncovered, until the cheese is firm and starting to turn golden brown, 15 to 20 minutes. If using store-bought cheese, remove from the oven once melted. Garnish with fresh basil before serving.

NUTRITION: 354.3 CALORIES   17.8g PROTEIN   45.5g CARBS   12.8g FAT   13.9g FIBER   4g SUGAR   310.1mg SODIUM

baked pumpkin sage risotto

I absolutely love risotto. It's one of the most delicious and comforting dishes ever created, but I don't love the tedious process of standing over the stove and stirring. Enter baked risotto! No endless stirring and standing. It turns out just as creamy, fabulous, and unbelievably delicious with this pumpkin and sage version.

1 cup (160g) finely diced red onion

5 large garlic cloves (15g), minced

2 tablespoons (6g) finely chopped fresh sage, plus more for garnish

1 tablespoon (2g) finely minced fresh rosemary, plus more for garnish

½ cup (120g) dry white wine

1½ cups (300g) Arborio rice

3½ cups (840g) low-sodium vegetable broth

1 cup (240g) cooked pumpkin puree (either canned or homemade)

2 tablespoons (16g) nutritional yeast or Lemon Parmesan Cheese (page 267)

1 teaspoon fine sea salt

NOTE While the wine in this risotto gives great flavor, if you don't consume any alcohol, you can replace the wine with ½ cup vegetable broth and 1 teaspoon rice vinegar.

1. Preheat the oven to 375°F.

2. In a large nonstick frying pan, combine the onion and ½ cup (120g) water and cook over medium heat until translucent, 5 to 8 minutes. Add the garlic and fresh herbs and cook another couple of minutes, stirring often. Add a splash of water as needed to prevent burning.

3. Add the wine and cook for a couple of minutes until it's almost gone. Add the rice and stir for a minute. Add the broth, pumpkin puree, nutritional yeast, and salt and stir very well until evenly mixed. Bring to a boil and then immediately remove from the heat.

4. Very carefully pour the risotto mixture into a deep 3-quart ceramic or porcelain baking dish. Spread out the top and cover with a lid or a piece of foil wrapped tightly.

5. Bake until the rice is tender and creamy, about 30 minutes. (That bake time was exactly perfect for me.)

6. Remove from the oven and give it a stir to mix the surrounding juices. Stir in some more sage or rosemary, if desired, or use as a beautiful garnish. Serve hot.

NUTRITION: 302.3 CALORIES   7.2g PROTEIN   60.9g CARBS   1.2g FAT   3.8g FIBER   6.3g SUGAR   422.4mg SODIUM

parmesan ratatouille

This dish is not only stunning with the vibrant colors of all of the vegetables, but it is packed with flavor and easy to make! It is incredibly comforting because it is filled with several veggies that are so beneficial to our health. It is filling, yet light and won't weigh you down. I always feel so good after eating roasted vegetables. The lemon parmesan cheese topping adds extra flavor and healthy fat and a great texture contrast to the juicy vegetables. The lemon flavor complements the bright flavors of the tomatoes so well. The herbes de Provence give the vegetables a lovely boost of flavor, so don't omit!

SAUCE

1 (14.5-ounce) can crushed fire-roasted tomatoes

1 teaspoon garlic powder

1 teaspoon herbes de Provence

1 teaspoon agave syrup

¼ teaspoon fine sea salt

VEGGIES

2 heaping cups (230g) sliced zucchini (cut into half-moons ¼ inch thick)

3 heaping cups (230g) sliced eggplant (cut into half-moons ¼ inch thick)

2 Roma tomatoes (250g), quartered

½ large red onion (100g), cut into 2-inch long slices

½ teaspoon fine sea salt

½ teaspoon herbes de Provence

½ cup (60g) Lemon Parmesan Cheese (page 267) or store-bought vegan parmesan

1. Preheat the oven to 375°F. Lightly mist a shallow 3-quart baking dish or a 9- or 10-inch round pie plate with cooking spray.

2. Make the sauce: In a medium bowl, combine the fire-roasted tomatoes, garlic powder, herbes de Provence, agave, and salt and stir until mixed. Spread at the bottom of the baking dish.

3. Prepare the veggies: In a large bowl, gently toss together the zucchini, eggplant, tomatoes, onion, salt, and herbes de Provence until mixed. Add these veggies on top of the tomato sauce in the baking dish in an even layer.

4. Cover with foil and bake for 30 minutes.

5. Remove the foil and bake until the veggies are fork-tender, another 20 minutes. Sprinkle the parmesan over the top and serve hot.

NUTRITION: 135 CALORIES   5.8g PROTEIN   18.3g CARBS   5g FAT   4.3g FIBER   9.1g SUGAR   735.2mg SODIUM

soul-satisfying soups

Creamy Mexican Potato and White Bean Soup _____ 122

Minestrone Soup with a Twist_____ 125

Veggie Pot Pie Soup_____ 128

Lentil Soup with Turmeric and Lemon _____ 131

Jackfruit Pinto Bean Chili _____ 134

Pureed Red Lentil Curry Kale Soup _____ 137

Feel-Good Roasted Red Pepper Veggie Soup _____ 140

Hungarian Bean Soup (Bab Leves) _____ 143

Comforting Sun-Dried Tomato and
Zucchini Lasagna Soup_____ 144

Tom Kha Soup with Tofu (Thai Coconut Soup)_____ 147

Miso Sweet Potato Kale Soup _____ 150

Smoky Red Lentil Soup _____ 153

creamy mexican potato and white bean soup

This soup has it all. If you are a fan of total comfort food, you will love this soup. It is creamy, chunky, spiced to perfection, and will keep you full for hours. Cashews make it so creamy and the potatoes and beans give such a hearty feeling in every bite. This is the kind of dish that will have your friends asking for the recipe. The soup comes together fairly quickly while cooking, so make sure to have all the veggies and spices measured and ready to go.

½ cup raw cashews (75g; see Note) or sunflower seeds (56g)

1 cup (160g) packed diced yellow or white onion

6 large garlic cloves (15g), minced

1 teaspoon onion powder

1 teaspoon garlic powder

1 teaspoon ground cumin

1 teaspoon dried oregano

½ teaspoon smoked paprika

½ teaspoon ground coriander

¾ teaspoon fine sea salt, plus more to taste

¼ teaspoon freshly ground black pepper

4 cups (840g) low-sodium vegetable broth

2 heaping cups (330g) ½-inch pieces peeled gold potatoes

1 (4-ounce) can green chiles

1 tablespoon (10g) finely minced pickled jalapeño (from a jar of mild or medium jalapeños)

2 (15-ounce) cans low-sodium white beans (510g), drained and rinsed

1 cup (140g) frozen sweet corn kernels

2 tablespoons (30g) fresh lime juice

Diced avocado and red pepper flakes (optional), for serving

1. In a high-powered blender, blend the cashews with ½ cup (120g) water until completely smooth and creamy. Set the cashew cream aside.

2. In a large pot, bring ½ cup (120g) water to a simmer over medium heat. Add the onion and sauté for 5 minutes. Add the garlic and cook for 1 more minute, adding tiny amounts of water if needed to prevent sticking or burning.

3. Add the onion powder, garlic powder, cumin, oregano, smoked paprika, coriander, salt, and black pepper and stir for about 30 seconds until fragrant.

4. Add the broth, potatoes, chiles, and jalapeños and bring to a boil. Stir well, reduce the heat to medium-low, and simmer until the potatoes are almost fully tender, 10 to 15 minutes.

recipe continues »

5. Add the beans, corn, reserved cashew cream, and lime juice. Stir well and cook until slightly thickened and the flavors develop more, 5 to 10 minutes. Taste and add salt if needed.

6. Serve with diced avocado and red pepper flakes, if desired.

NOTE   If you do not have a high-powered blender (such as a Vitamix), you need to soak the cashews in a bowl of water to cover overnight. Alternatively, you can cover the cashews in water in a saucepan and boil for 15 minutes. When ready to cook, drain and process in a food processor (I find a processor works better if you don't have a strong blender).

NUTRITION: 487.4 CALORIES   20.8g PROTEIN   81.8g CARBS   10.8g FAT   14.4g FIBER   11.7g SUGAR   558.5mg SODIUM

minestrone soup
with a twist

I've never been a big fan of classic minestrone soup because I always found it too watery, bland, and, well, a little on the boring side. So this is my version of minestrone with a much thicker soup base, deeper flavor, and, of course, the unexpected ingredients of chipotles and almond butter! Top it with my homemade parmesan for the ultimate minestrone soup experience.

1 cup (160g) finely diced white onion

2 teaspoons salt-free Italian seasoning or see Notes

2 teaspoons garlic powder

4 cups (960g) low-sodium vegetable broth

2 cups (480g) plain tomato sauce/passata

2 tablespoons (30g) chipotle peppers in adobo sauce, chopped

2 tablespoons (32g) creamy roasted almond butter (with no added oils/sugar)

1 tablespoon (20g) maple syrup or agave syrup

¾ teaspoon fine sea salt, plus more to taste

¼ teaspoon freshly ground black pepper

1 cup (140g) elbow macaroni (use gluten-free if needed)

1 cup (170g) cooked white beans

1 cup (170g) frozen mixed veggies

½ cup Lemon Parmesan Cheese (page 267; optional), for serving

Fresh basil (optional), for garnish

1. In a large pot, combine ½ cup (120g) water and the onion and cook over medium heat, stirring occasionally, until translucent, about 5 minutes.

2. Add the Italian seasoning and garlic powder and stir for 30 seconds to toast the spices. Add the vegetable broth, tomato sauce, chipotles, almond butter, maple syrup, salt, and pepper and stir really well, making sure the almond butter is thoroughly mixed.

3. Add the pasta, increase the heat to high, and bring to a boil. Once boiling, reduce the heat to low and simmer for about 5 minutes. Add the beans and veggie mix and cook until the pasta is tender, but not mushy, another 5 minutes or so.

recipe continues »

4. Taste and add more salt, if needed (the amount can vary based on the broth and tomato sauce used). If desired, top with lemon parmesan and basil for the full minestrone soup experience!

NOTES
- Use gluten-free lentil or chickpea pasta for a higher protein option.
- While I recommend chipotles in adobe sauce, you can sub in ¼ teaspoon chipotle chile powder and ½ teaspoon smoked paprika for a similar result.
- If you don't have Italian seasoning, sub in 1 teaspoon each dried basil and oregano.

NUTRITION: 455.1 CALORIES   17.1g PROTEIN   84.4g CARBS   6.8g FAT   12.2g FIBER   18.9g SUGAR   644.1mg SODIUM

veggie pot pie soup

Who doesn't love a classic pot pie?? I've eaten many pot pies in my life, and they are so comforting. They can be a bit more work, though, so enter pot pie soup! This soup relies on the flavor of the miso and my homemade poultry seasoning for that signature pot pie flavor, so do not omit or it will be bland. Make sure to use a well-flavored broth here: I prefer broths from Sprouts, Pacific, and Imagine.

½ cup (75g) raw cashews (see Notes)

1 tablespoon (20g) red miso

3½ cups (840g) low-sodium vegetable broth

1 cup (160g) packed diced yellow onion

Fine sea salt

1 tablespoon (15g) minced garlic

1 tablespoon Poultry Seasoning (page 260) or salt-free store-bought (see Notes)

3 heaping cups (480g) ½-inch pieces peeled gold potatoes

⅛ teaspoon freshly ground black pepper, plus more to taste

2¼ cups (285g) frozen carrots and peas mix

1 (10-inch) flour tortilla, torn into large chip-size pieces (use gluten-free if desired)

2 to 3 tablespoons chopped fresh parsley (optional), for garnish

1. Preheat the oven to 400°F. Line a sheet pan with parchment paper.

2. In a high-powered blender, combine the cashews, ¾ cup (180g) water, and the miso and blend until completely smooth. Set the cashew/miso milk aside.

3. In a large pot, bring ½ cup (120g) of the broth to a simmer over medium heat. Add the onion and a pinch of salt and cook, stirring occasionally, until tender, about 8 minutes.

4. Add the garlic and cook another 1 to 2 minutes, adding a touch more broth if needed. Add the poultry seasoning and stir for about 30 seconds to absorb any residual moisture and to toast it. This will release the seasoning's aroma and bring out its flavor.

5. Add the potatoes, the remaining 3 cups of broth, ¾ teaspoon salt, and the pepper. Stir well and bring to a boil. Reduce the heat to medium-low, cover, and cook for about 5 minutes or until the potatoes are almost fully tender.

recipe continues »

6. Stir in the cashew/miso milk and carrots and peas mix. Return to a boil, then reduce the heat to low and simmer, uncovered, until the veggies are tender and the soup has thickened nicely, about 10 minutes. Taste and add more salt and/or pepper, if desired.

7. Meanwhile, spread the tortilla pieces on the lined sheet pan and bake until golden brown on the edges, 4 to 5 minutes. Watch closely so they don't burn. Cook time can vary depending on the type of tortilla used.

8. Ladle into serving bowls and garnish with fresh parsley, if desired. Divide the tortilla pieces among the bowls of soup.

NOTES

- Use sunflower seeds (56g) instead of cashews for a nut-free option, but note that the flavor will be a bit different and not quite as neutral or creamy.
- If you do not have a high-powered blender (such as a Vitamix), you need to soak the cashews in a bowl of water to cover overnight. When ready to cook, drain and process in a food processor (which works better than a weak blender).
- DO NOT use a store-bought cashew milk—it will be very watery and not thicken or taste right at all.
- Although I love my homemade poultry seasoning, if you use store-bought, make sure to use a salt-free blend. I love the Spice Hunter brand (one with the added onion/garlic). I don't recommend the McCormick brand, though, as it's too heavy on the sage and will turn the soup green.

NUTRITION: 524.1 CALORIES   15.4g PROTEIN   85.8g CARBS   15.8g FAT   12.2g FIBER   14.3g SUGAR   1098.2mg SODIUM

lentil soup with turmeric and lemon

This soup is by far one of the most popular recipes I've ever written. It also happens to be high protein and I had some readers request that it be put in this book, so here we are! It has a perfect 5-star rating on my blog for many reasons: It has delicious subtle touches of ginger, turmeric, and lemon for a bright but warming flavor and it's incredibly creamy and dreamy in every bite. Have all your ingredients measured and ready to go since the soup comes together pretty quickly.

½ cup raw cashews (75g; see Note) or sunflower seeds (56g)

4½ cups (1,080g) low-sodium vegetable broth (I love Pacific and Imagine brands), plus more as needed

1 cup (160g) finely diced yellow onion

5 large garlic cloves (15g), minced

1 heaping cup (150g) ¼-inch sliced carrots

2 teaspoons garlic powder

2 teaspoons onion powder

1 teaspoon ground ginger

½ teaspoon ground turmeric

1¼ teaspoons fine sea salt, plus more to taste

¼ teaspoon freshly ground black pepper, plus more to taste

1½ cups (280g) green lentils, rinsed

2 teaspoons maple syrup or agave syrup

2 tablespoons (30g) fresh lemon juice, plus more (optional) for serving

4 large handfuls of fresh spinach (80g)

Lemon slices (optional), for garnish

1. In a high-powered blender, combine the cashews and 1 cup (240g) water and blend until completely smooth. Set the cashew cream aside.

2. In a large pot, bring ½ cup (120g) of the broth to a simmer over medium heat. Once hot, add the onions and cook, stirring a bit, until soft, about 5 minutes.

3. Add the garlic and carrots and cook until the carrots are mostly tender, but not fully, 3 to 5 minutes. Add small amounts of broth as needed to prevent sticking.

4. Add the garlic powder, onion powder, ginger, turmeric, salt, and pepper and stir for about 30 seconds. Add the rinsed lentils, the remaining 4 cups (950g) of broth, and the maple syrup. Stir well and bring to a boil over high heat. Once at a boil, reduce the

recipe continues »

heat to low, partially cover (just allowing a small amount of steam to escape), and simmer until the lentils are tender to your liking, about 20 minutes.

5. Add the cashew cream, lemon juice, and spinach and stir through. Cook for about 5 minutes to thicken it a bit and wilt the spinach.

6. Taste the soup. Add more salt and/or pepper if needed. This amount can really vary depending on the broth used. Mine needed another good pinch. The lemon should be noticeable, but not overpowering. The lemon flavor does settle down after sitting out. If you'd like more, add more lemon juice to the serving bowls and/or garnish with lemon slices. I like to add extra freshly ground black pepper on top for serving.

NOTE If you do not have a high-powered blender (such as a Vitamix), you need to soak the cashews in a bowl of water to cover overnight. When ready to cook, drain and process in a food processor (which works better than a weak blender).

NUTRITION: 365.9 CALORIES   16.8g PROTEIN   61.3g CARBS   7.4g FAT   9.1g FIBER   10.6g SUGAR   553.1mg SODIUM

jackfruit pinto bean chili

This jackfruit bean chili has a wonderful "shredded chicken" texture thanks to the jackfruit, which is first baked and then cooked again in the chili. Jackfruit can be a bit too soft for my liking, but cooking it twice solves the problem and yields a wonderful, meaty texture. This chili has so many warming spices and fresh veggies for a delicious comforting meal with lots of flavor!

JACKFRUIT

1 (20-ounce) can young green jackfruit in brine, drained (I use Trader Joe's)

½ teaspoon liquid smoke

½ teaspoon ground cumin

1 teaspoon chili powder

½ teaspoon garlic powder

¼ teaspoon fine sea salt

CHILI

4¼ cups (1,020g) low-sodium vegetable broth

1 cup (160g) finely chopped yellow onion

1 tablespoon (15g) minced garlic

1 cup (160g) chopped green bell pepper

½ cup (64g) chopped poblano pepper

1 jalapeño, finely chopped

1 tablespoon chili powder

1 tablespoon ground cumin

1 teaspoon ground coriander

2 teaspoons garlic powder

¼ teaspoon freshly ground black pepper

1 teaspoon fine sea salt, plus more to taste

1 (15-ounce) can pinto beans, drained and rinsed, or 1½ cups (255g) cooked beans

1 cup (140g) frozen sweet corn kernels

1 teaspoon liquid smoke

1 tablespoon (20g) pure maple syrup

1 tablespoon (15g) fresh lime juice

Diced avocado (optional), for serving

Vegan sour cream (optional), for serving

Cilantro (optional), for garnish

1. Prepare the jackfruit: Preheat the oven to 375°F. Line a sheet pan with parchment paper.

2. In a bowl, use two forks to shred the drained jackfruit thoroughly like shredded chicken. For the tougher chunks, use a knife to slice it. This process will take several minutes, so be patient.

3. Add the shredded jackfruit to a sieve and place paper towels on top to press and squeeze out extra liquid. The drier the jackfruit, the better the result for a chicken-like texture in the final dish.

recipe continues »

4. Add the liquid smoke, cumin, chili powder, garlic powder, and salt to the jackfruit and mix until well coated. Spread out on the lined pan.

5. Bake for 30 minutes.

6. Meanwhile, start the chili: In a large pot, bring ½ cup (120g) of the broth to a simmer over medium heat. Once simmering, add the onion and cook, stirring occasionally, until tender, about 5 minutes.

7. Add another ¼ cup (60g) of the broth, the garlic, bell pepper, poblano pepper, and jalapeño. Cook, stirring often, until tender, 5 to 8 minutes. Add more broth if needed.

8. Add the chili powder, cumin, coriander, garlic powder, black pepper, and salt and stir for about 30 seconds to absorb any residual moisture and to toast them and bring out their flavor. Add the remaining 3½ cups (840g) of broth, the pinto beans, corn, liquid smoke, maple syrup, and lime juice. Stir in the baked jackfruit. Stir well and bring back to a boil. Once boiling, reduce the heat to low and simmer about 10 minutes.

9. Taste and add more salt if needed (this amount can vary depending on the broth used). Top each serving with avocado and vegan sour cream, if desired, for a touch of creaminess and garnish with cilantro, if using.

NUTRITION: 365.5 CALORIES   12g PROTEIN   71.2g CARBS   4.5g FAT   17.5g FIBER   18.7g SUGAR   1093.2mg SODIUM

pureed red lentil curry kale soup

This soup will have you dreaming about making it over and over. It warms you up and is so comforting. I was just smiling while eating a bowl. It's smooth, creamy, extremely flavorful, and so easy to make. The fresh herbs complete it with an extra touch of flavor. For the curry powder, you can use a store-bought version or my homemade version. I love using lentils in recipes for their amazing protein content, versatility, and ability to take on an array of different flavors.

1 cup (160g) finely diced white onion

4 large garlic cloves (12g), minced

1½ teaspoons yellow curry powder, homemade (see page 259) or store-bought

½ teaspoon garam masala

2 tablespoons (30g) tomato paste

1½ cups (300g) red lentils (see Note), rinsed well

4 cups (960g) low-sodium vegetable broth

¾ teaspoon fine sea salt, plus more to taste

¼ teaspoon freshly ground black pepper

¼ teaspoon red pepper flakes

1 cup (240g) canned unsweetened "lite" coconut milk

2 tablespoons (30g) fresh lime juice, plus more to taste

2 large handfuls of fresh kale (45g), roughly chopped

3 tablespoons (9g) finely chopped fresh cilantro

3 tablespoons (9g) finely chopped fresh mint

1. In a large pot, bring ½ cup (120g) water to a simmer over medium heat. Add the onion and cook, stirring occasionally, until translucent, about 5 minutes. Add the garlic and cook another couple of minutes, adding water if needed to prevent burning. Add the curry powder, garam masala, and tomato paste and stir for a minute. Add the lentils, broth, salt, black pepper, and pepper flakes and stir well. Bring to a boil over high heat. Reduce the heat to low, partially cover to allow some steam to escape, and simmer until the lentils are fully tender, about 10 minutes.

2. Add the coconut milk and lime juice and simmer for about 5 minutes to heat through. Remove from the heat. Using an

recipe continues »

immersion blender, carefully blend to a smooth consistency (or transfer to a stand blender, blend, and return to the pot). Blending the soup makes it creamier and really allows all the flavors to meld together.

3. Add the kale and cook over low heat until the kale is tender to your liking, about 5 minutes. The soup will thicken a bit more, too. Add the cilantro and mint. Taste and add more salt if needed and lime juice if you want it tangier.

NOTES
- It is important to use only red lentils here, as they cook much quicker than all other lentil varieties. The recipe would not work the same if red lentils were substituted.
- Please be careful when blending hot liquids. Make sure the lid is secure and always use an oven mitt.

NUTRITION: 544.8 CALORIES   24.2g PROTEIN   83.9g CARBS   16.7g FAT   14.2g FIBER   13g SUGAR   544.8mg SODIUM

feel-good roasted red pepper veggie soup

I love how light this soup is, yet so wonderfully filling. I fell in love with it when I tested it. It's a delicious nod to Southwestern flavors. The base is unique, as we are roasting red bell peppers first and using that as the base of the soup, as opposed to all broth. It is the perfect soup to warm your body on a chilly evening. I like serving it with sliced avocado for an added healthy fat, and red pepper flakes.

2 medium red bell peppers (13 ounces/374g total)

4 cups (960g) low-sodium vegetable broth

1 teaspoon onion powder

1 teaspoon chili powder

1 teaspoon ground cumin

½ teaspoon smoked paprika

¾ teaspoon fine sea salt, plus more to taste

¼ teaspoon freshly ground black pepper

2 heaping cups (330g) ¾-inch pieces peeled gold potatoes

2 cups (7 ounces/200g) cauliflower florets

1 (15-ounce) can low-sodium black beans, drained and rinsed, or 1½ cups (255g) cooked beans

1 cup (240g) unsweetened creamy plant-based milk (I used almond)

2 tablespoons (30g) fresh lime juice

2 tablespoons (30g) tomato paste

2 large handfuls of kale (60g), roughly chopped

1 cup (140g) frozen sweet corn kernels

1 tablespoon (20g) pure maple syrup or agave syrup

1. Preheat the oven to 425°F. Line a sheet pan with parchment.

2. Set the whole peppers on the pan and roast until well charred, about 25 minutes.

3. Meanwhile, in a large pot, combine the broth, onion powder, chili powder, cumin, smoked paprika, salt, and black pepper and stir well. Add the potatoes and bring to a boil. Reduce the heat to medium and simmer for about 5 minutes. Add the cauliflower and beans and cook until the potatoes are tender, another 5 minutes.

4. When the peppers are cool enough to handle, stem and seed them and add them to a blender. Add the milk, lime juice, and tomato paste and blend until completely smooth.

5. Add the pureed red pepper mixture, kale, corn, and maple syrup to the pot and stir well. Heat through for a couple of minutes to marry all the ingredients. Taste and adjust the salt, if needed.

NUTRITION: 348.5 CALORIES   13.4g PROTEIN   70.5g CARBS   3.5g FAT   13.7g FIBER   17.9g SUGAR   618mg SODIUM

hungarian bean soup (bab leves)

If you love beans and smoky flavors, this soup is for you! This recipe was inspired by my bachata dance teacher, Barnabas Vadon, who is Hungarian and shared this recipe with me. The original recipe is not vegan, so I made many changes to make up for the lack of meat. The classic recipe uses ham hock and is quite smoky. To mimic those flavors, I used smoked paprika, liquid smoke, and a touch of maple syrup. If you really want to amp up the smoky flavor and protein content, add my All-Purpose Smoky Tofu (page 277) at the end of cooking just to heat through.

1½ cups (200g) finely chopped white onion

6 large garlic cloves (22g), minced

1 teaspoon Hungarian paprika

½ teaspoon smoked paprika

1 teaspoon fine sea salt, plus more to taste

¼ teaspoon freshly ground black pepper, plus more to taste

2 large carrots (3 to 4 ounces/ 100g total), peeled and sliced ¼ inch thick

4 cups (960g) low-sodium vegetable broth

2 teaspoons liquid smoke

2 fresh bay leaves (not dried)

2 (15-ounce) cans low-sodium small white beans or navy beans, drained and rinsed, or 3 cups (510g) cooked beans

2 teaspoons pure maple syrup

¼ cup (60g) plain nondairy yogurt

1 teaspoon rice vinegar

3 tablespoons (9g) chopped fresh parsley

Red pepper flakes (optional), for garnish

Fresh bread (optional), for serving

NOTE This soup is good the first day, but I strongly recommend, if possible, making it the day ahead of when you plan to serve it. The flavors intensify so beautifully overnight and just taste amazing!

1. In a large pot, bring ½ cup (120g) water to a simmer over medium heat. Add the onion and cook, stirring occasionally, until tender, about 8 minutes. Add the garlic and cook another couple of minutes.

2. Add both paprikas, the salt, black pepper, carrots, broth, liquid smoke, and bay leaves. Stir well and bring to a boil. Reduce the heat to medium-low and gently simmer for 5 minutes. Add the beans and maple syrup and simmer until the carrots are tender, another 5 minutes or so.

3. Add the yogurt and vinegar and heat through for a couple of minutes. Taste and add more salt or pepper, if needed. Add the parsley, garnish with the red pepper flakes (if using), and serve immediately. I love to serve this with fresh bread.

NUTRITION: 469.5 CALORIES   22.1g PROTEIN   91.2g CARBS   3.2g FAT   17g FIBER   16.4g SUGAR   901mg SODIUM

comforting sun-dried tomato and zucchini lasagna soup

This soup is comfort in a bowl. It is a unique twist on a classic tomato soup with the satisfying texture of a lasagna. The sun-dried tomatoes give a wonderful punch of flavor and tang that is balanced by the creaminess of the cashews and tahini. With fresh spinach and basil, it is a soup that has it all. You can substitute sunflower seeds if you're allergic to cashews. If you would like to make this a more chunky and higher protein soup, add one 15-ounce can of drained chickpeas at the time of adding the spinach. Use lentil lasagna for even more protein! Prep time does not include soaking the tomatoes.

¼ cup (26g) dry-pack sun-dried tomatoes (not oil-packed)

¼ cup raw cashews (40g; see Note) or sunflower seeds (36g)

5½ cups (1,320g) low-sodium vegetable broth

2 tablespoons (32g) tahini (see Note page 206)

1 tablespoon (15g) red wine vinegar

1 cup (240g) plain tomato sauce/passata

5 extra-large garlic cloves (16g), minced

2 teaspoons onion powder

1 teaspoon garlic powder

2 teaspoons salt-free Italian seasoning

1 large (or 2 small) zucchini (11 ounces/316g), cut into bite-size chunks

½ teaspoon fine sea salt, plus more to taste

6 lasagna sheets (use gluten-free if needed), each broken into fourths

⅛ teaspoon cayenne pepper, plus more to taste

2 large handfuls of fresh spinach (75g)

2 handfuls of fresh basil leaves (12g), roughly chopped

Red pepper flakes, for garnish

1. Add the sundried tomatoes to a bowl and fill with boiling water. Soak the tomatoes for 30 minutes to soften them so they're easier to blend. Drain and proceed with the recipe.

2. In a high-powered blender, combine the cashews, soaked sun-dried tomatoes, 1 cup (240g) of the broth, the tahini, vinegar, and tomato sauce. Blend until completely smooth and creamy with no bits of nuts remaining. You will need to scrape down the sides a few times in between blending. It should be thick, creamy, and completely smooth. Set aside.

recipe continues »

3. In a large pot, heat a few tablespoons water over medium heat. Add the garlic and sauté for a couple of minutes. Add the onion powder, garlic powder, and Italian seasoning and stir for about a minute.

4. Stir in the zucchini, ¼ teaspoon of the salt, and 1 cup (240g) of the broth. Bring to a simmer, cover, reduce the heat to medium-low, and cook until the zucchini starts to become tender, about 3 minutes.

5. Add the lasagna pasta and remaining 3½ cups (840g) of broth and raise the heat to medium. Simmer until the pasta is al dente, 7 to 10 minutes. The zucchini should be tender by now as well.

6. Stir in the reserved sun-dried tomato sauce. Add the cayenne, the remaining ¼ teaspoon of salt, and the spinach. Heat through just for a couple of minutes to wilt the spinach. The soup will thicken over the next several minutes and the longer it sits, the more the pasta will absorb the liquid.

7. Remove from the heat and taste to see if more salt is needed (the sun-dried tomatoes and tomato sauce give a great punch of flavor, so mine did not need any). If you'd like it spicier, add more cayenne.

8. Add the fresh basil and pepper flakes right before serving.

NOTE If you do not have a high-powered blender (such as a Vitamix), you need to soak the cashews in a bowl of water to cover overnight. Alternatively, you can cover the cashews in water in a saucepan and boil for 15 minutes. When ready to cook, drain and process in a food processor (which works better than a weak blender).

NUTRITION: 444.7 CALORIES   15g PROTEIN   74.1g CARBS   12.3g FAT   9.2g FIBER   17.6g SUGAR   504mg SODIUM

tom kha soup with tofu (thai coconut soup)

This recipe was a request from my longtime reader Micah, so I had to honor the request! Traditional tom kha gai soup is a Thai coconut chicken soup that is spicy, sour, rich, and creamy from full-fat coconut milk, with a subtle sweetness. It is made with specific ingredients like galangal, lemongrass, makrut lime leaves, and chicken. My version is inspired by the traditional recipe, but without those exact ingredients. Instead, I used very similar flavors, and to me, it still turned out a huge winner!

I cannot stress enough that you should make this soup the day before you want to eat it! It is good when first made, but the flavors marry incredibly overnight and take on a much deeper flavor, so I strongly encourage making it the day before.

20 ounces extra-firm tofu (see Notes)

½ cup (80g) finely chopped white onion

2 tablespoons (18g) minced garlic

1 tablespoon (13g) minced fresh ginger

1 to 3 green Thai chile peppers, to taste, sliced

1 cup (80g) sliced baby bella mushrooms

3 mini red sweet bell peppers, sliced (85g)

4 cups (960g) low-sodium quality vegetable broth

1 tablespoon (15g) vegan Thai red curry paste

3 tablespoons (45g) reduced-sodium soy sauce

2 tablespoons (40g) agave syrup

1 (13.6-ounce) can unsweetened full-fat coconut milk (do not use "lite" here!)

½ teaspoon fine sea salt, plus more to taste

2 tablespoons (30g) fresh lime juice, plus more to taste

Optional garnish: Fresh cilantro and green onions

1. Press the tofu (see Notes) and let sit for about 15 minutes. Then cut into ½-inch cubes.

2. Meanwhile, in a large pot, bring ½ cup (120g) water to a simmer over medium heat. Add the onion and sauté until translucent, about 5 minutes. Add the garlic, ginger, and chiles (I used 3 because I wanted a nice kick) and cook for another couple of minutes. Add the mushrooms, bell peppers, and another splash of water as needed just to prevent sticking or burning and cook until the veggies are softened, about 5 minutes.

recipe continues »

3. Stir in the broth, tofu, curry paste, soy sauce, agave, coconut milk, and salt. Bring to a boil. Reduce the heat to medium-low and simmer for 10 minutes. Add the lime juice and heat through for 1 minute.

4. I highly recommend letting the soup sit overnight before eating for the flavors to intensify, as well as blend into a deep, well-balanced flavor. At the very least, it should sit for a couple of hours. But if you just can't wait, let the soup sit 10 minutes, taste, and add more salt and/or lime juice if needed. If desired, garnish with fresh cilantro and green onions.

NOTES

- To press tofu: Use a tofu press if you have one. Otherwise, place several layers of paper towel on a large plate or cutting board. Set the tofu on the paper towels and top the tofu with more paper towels. Place a weight (like a skillet filled with canned goods) on top to help press the water out of the tofu.
- If you do not eat tofu, you can sub in 1 or 2 cans of drained chickpeas depending on if you want the soup to be thicker with lots of chickpeas or more brothy with only one can.

NUTRITION: 554.6 CALORIES   21.9g PROTEIN   49.8g CARBS   32g FAT   7.7g FIBER   20.1g SUGAR   849.8mg SODIUM

miso sweet potato kale soup

Feeling under the weather? This soup is just what you need. It is full of nutritious vitamin-packed veggies and a warming broth with the umami of miso. It has a spicy kick from the Thai chiles that will warm you throughout your body. If you are sensitive to heat, use only 1 chile pepper or a small amount of jalapeño instead.

1 cup (160g) finely chopped white onion

5 large garlic cloves, minced (15g)

1 inch piece ginger, finely grated (10g)

1 to 2 green Thai chile peppers, to taste, sliced

2 to 3 tablespoons (30g to 45g) red miso

½ teaspoon ground coriander

5 cups (1,200g) low-sodium vegetable broth

5 cups (630g) peeled and chopped sweet potatoes in ¾ inch pieces

1 (15-ounce) can low-sodium chickpeas, drained and rinsed, or 1½ cups (255g) cooked chickpeas

½ cup (120g) plain tomato sauce/passata

½ teaspoon fine sea salt, plus more to taste

4 handfuls of kale (90g), roughly chopped

½ cup (44g) sliced green onions, for garnish

1. In a large pot, bring ½ cup (120g) water to a simmer over medium heat. Add the onion and sauté until tender, about 5 minutes. Add the garlic, ginger, and chile peppers (use only 1 if you don't like it too spicy). Cook another couple of minutes, adding a splash of water if needed to prevent sticking and burning.

2. Add 2 tablespoons of the miso, the coriander, and ½ cup (120g) of the broth and stir until all the miso is dissolved. Add the sweet potatoes and remaining 4½ cups (1,000g) of broth and bring to a boil. Reduce the heat to medium-low and simmer until the sweet potatoes are almost fully tender, about 10 minutes.

3. Add the chickpeas, tomato sauce, and salt. Stir well and simmer until the sweet potatoes are tender, another 5 minutes.

4. Stir in the kale and heat through for a couple of minutes until just tender. Taste and add more salt or another tablespoon of miso, if desired (this amount can vary based on the broth and tomato sauce used).

5. Serve garnished with the green onions.

NUTRITION: 419.1 CALORIES   14.1g PROTEIN   84.6g CARBS   4.1g FAT   14.5g FIBER   20.5g SUGAR   804.1mg SODIUM

smoky red lentil soup

This smoky red lentil soup is high in protein, fast, easy, simple, and delicious! I love making recipes with red lentils because they cook in under 10 minutes and can take on any flavor profile you like. This soup has lots of spices and tangy ingredients to please the palate. Lentils don't taste like much on their own, so adding lots of flavor is important. The tomato paste and lemon juice are super important here for finishing it off! This recipe also makes a large pot, so you can enjoy leftovers.

6 cups (1,440g) low-sodium vegetable broth

1 cup (160g) diced red bell pepper

2 teaspoons smoked paprika

1 teaspoon garlic powder

1 teaspoon onion powder

1 teaspoon chili powder

¼ teaspoon red pepper flakes, plus extra for garnish

2 cups (400g) red lentils, rinsed well

1 teaspoon fine sea salt, plus more to taste

¼ teaspoon freshly ground black pepper

¼ cup (60g) tomato paste

2 tablespoons (30g) fresh lemon juice, plus more to taste

3 large handfuls of fresh spinach (100g)

½ cup sliced green onions, for garnish

1. In a large pot, bring ½ cup (120g) of the broth to a simmer over medium heat. Once simmering, add the bell pepper and simmer for 5 minutes. Add the smoked paprika, garlic powder, onion powder, chili powder, and pepper flakes and stir for 30 seconds until the mixture smells fragrant and has absorbed any residual liquid.

2. Add the lentils, the remaining 5½ cups (1,320g) of broth, the salt, and black pepper and bring to a boil. Reduce the heat to low, partially cover (to allow steam to escape), and simmer until the lentils are at your desired texture, 8 to 10 minutes (I like 8 minutes). Red lentils cook very quickly, so don't overcook them or they'll get mushy.

3. Add the tomato paste, lemon juice, and spinach and stir until all of the tomato paste is dissolved throughout the soup. Taste and season with more lemon juice and salt, if needed (this will depend on which broth was used).

4. Serve garnished with the green onions and red pepper flakes for an extra kick.

NUTRITION: 575 CALORIES   31.2g PROTEIN   109.3g CARBS   3.5g FAT   17.3g FIBER   16.1g SUGAR   776.2mg SODIUM

wholesome and hearty mains

Veggie-Packed Lentil Rice Patties _____ 156

Rosemary-Infused Sweet Potato Tofu Patties _____ 159

Protein-Packed Mac 'n' Cheese _____ 162

Thai Green Sweet Potato Curry _____ 165

Sweet and Sour Tofu with Ramen _____ 168

Guestworthy Jackfruit Lentil Curry _____ 171

Sweet Potato Curry Pasta _____ 174

Harissa Almond Pasta with Spinach _____ 177

Swedish Meatballs _____ 178

BBQ Jackfruit Cheese Pizzas _____ 181

Cheesy Quinoa Poblano Peppers _____ 183

Teriyaki Stuffed Bell Peppers _____ 187

Cajun Spinach Artichoke Pasta _____ 188

veggie-packed lentil rice patties

These patties are packed with veggies and so much flavor. The spices and lime juice are perfectly balanced with the sweetness of the corn. The texture is hearty and satisfying. The combo of lentils and rice makes these patties a complete protein. These can be served alongside a salad, a sweet potato, or as mini burger sliders. I love to serve them with my lime yogurt chive sauce.

½ cup (80g) packed finely diced red onion

1 small jalapeño (20g) finely diced

½ cup (80g) finely diced red bell pepper

1 teaspoon fine sea salt

1 teaspoon garlic powder

1 teaspoon onion powder

½ teaspoon ground cumin

1 (15-ounce) can low-sodium lentils, drained and rinsed

⅔ cup (108g) cooked white rice, cooled

2 tablespoons (30g) fresh lime juice

½ cup (75g) sweet corn kernels (I used frozen)

¼ cup (32g) oat flour (gluten-free if needed)

Lime Yogurt Chive Sauce (page 255; optional, see Note), for serving

1. In a large nonstick frying pan, bring ¼ cup (60g) water to a simmer over medium heat. Add the onion, jalapeño, bell pepper, and ¼ teaspoon of the salt and sauté until tender, 5 to 8 minutes. Add a splash of water as needed to prevent sticking. Add the garlic powder, onion powder, and cumin and toast for 30 seconds. Remove from the heat.

2. Preheat the oven to 400°F. Line a sheet pan with parchment paper.

3. In a food processor, combine the cooked veggie mixture, lentils, rice, lime juice, corn, oat flour, and the remaining ¾ teaspoon of salt. Pulse a few times until all the ingredients are roughly combined into a thick sticky mixture, but do not puree it. You still want lots of texture. The mixture will be quite damp, but it will firm up beautifully during baking.

4. Use a ⅓-cup measure (or weigh 90g) and form into 6 round patties. They should be flattened to about 1 inch thick.

recipe continues »

5. Place the patties on the lined sheet pan and bake for 25 minutes.

6. At this point, they should flip over easily. Use a thin spatula to flip them, not your hands, or they might break. If they are sticking to the paper still, cook a few minutes longer before flipping. Bake until golden brown on the second side, about 10 minutes.

7. Serve with the lime yogurt chive sauce.

NOTE   While I love to serve these with the lime yogurt chive sauce, in a pinch, a squeeze of lime juice also gives a nice boost of flavor. Even a salsa would complement the spices and flavors in the patties.

NUTRITION (1 patty): 153.2 CALORIES   7g PROTEIN   30g CARBS   0.9g FAT   4.6g FIBER   2.2g SUGAR   327.9mg SODIUM

rosemary-infused sweet potato tofu patties

These patties are going to give you serious fall and Thanksgiving vibes, from the fresh rosemary taste and aroma to the sweet potatoes! Crumbling the tofu gives some seriously amazing meaty texture to these patties. They taste fresh and full of flavor and, while good on their own, they are next level when served with my rosemary lemon cream.

14 ounces extra-firm tofu

½ cup (120g) mashed cooked sweet potato (see Note, page 225)

2 teaspoons finely chopped fresh rosemary

1 teaspoon garlic powder

1 teaspoon onion powder

½ teaspoon dried oregano

2 tablespoons (30g) coconut aminos

1 tablespoon (15g) fresh lemon juice

1 teaspoon fine sea salt

¼ teaspoon freshly ground black pepper

½ cup (36g) panko bread crumbs (use gluten-free if needed)

3 tablespoons (24g) cornstarch

1 large handful (25g) fresh spinach, roughly chopped

Rosemary Lemon Cream (page 244; optional), for serving

1. Press the tofu (see Note) and let sit for about 15 minutes. This step is very important to keep the tofu from tasting bland. Since the tofu will be crumbled for this recipe, at this point, I use several layers of paper towels to wrap up the pressed block of tofu and squeeze the water out multiple times until it is really dry. I do this over a sieve and it makes the process easier.

2. Preheat the oven to 375°F. Line a sheet pan with parchment paper.

3. Break up the tofu into small, crumbled pieces with your hands into a large bowl. Add the mashed sweet potato, rosemary, garlic powder, onion powder, oregano, coconut aminos, lemon juice, salt, and pepper. Use a fork to mash all the ingredients together until well mixed.

recipe continues »

4. Add the panko, cornstarch, and spinach and use your hands to press the mixture so it holds together in between your hands. This step must be done with your hands, as the fork will not cause the mixture to come together. Do this for a few minutes until it's evenly mixed.

5. Pack the mixture into a ¼-cup measure to form into 8 round patties. They should be flattened to about 1 inch thick and 2 to 3 inches wide. Arrange the patties on the lined pan.

6. Bake the first side for 30 minutes.

7. Flip carefully and bake until golden brown, another 10 to 15 minutes.

8. To enhance the overall rosemary flavor, serve with the rosemary lemon cream, if desired.

NOTE To press tofu: Use a tofu press if you have one. Otherwise, place several layers of paper towel on a large plate or cutting board. Set the tofu on the paper towels and top with more paper towels. Place a weight (like a skillet filled with canned goods) on top to help press the water out of the tofu.

NUTRITION (1 patty): 94.5 CALORIES   6g PROTEIN   11.6g CARBS   2.6g FAT   1.4g FIBER   1.7g SUGAR   374.3mg SODIUM

protein-packed mac 'n' cheese

I have a mac 'n' cheese recipe in my first cookbook that is really good, but this one takes the cake! It is so rich, creamy, decadent, and cheesy—a real winner. My daughter constantly requests it! Who says mac 'n' cheese has to be unhealthy, fattening, and loaded with dairy to be good? This version is full of wholesome ingredients, with no oil, butter, or fake processed cheese. It also has a good dose of protein from tofu. But don't worry, you don't taste the tofu.

¼ cup (60g) firm tofu (see Notes)

12 ounces elbow macaroni (use gluten-free if needed)

1 cup (240g) low-sodium vegetable broth

6 tablespoons (90g) plain nondairy yogurt

½ cup (75g) raw cashews (see Notes)

1 cup (240g) mashed cooked gold potato

1 tablespoon (15g) distilled white vinegar

1½ teaspoons fresh lemon juice

2 teaspoons white or red miso

2 tablespoons (16g) nutritional yeast or Lemon Parmesan Cheese (page 267)

Freshly ground black pepper

1 teaspoon fine sea salt, plus more to taste

⅓ cup (25g) panko bread crumbs (use gluten-free if needed)

½ teaspoon paprika

1. Press the tofu (see Notes) for 15 minutes.

2. Bring a large pot of water to a boil. Salt the water well, add the pasta, and cook until al dente according to the package directions. Drain the pasta, but do not rinse, and return to the pot.

3. Preheat the oven to 350°F.

4. Meanwhile, in a high-powered blender, combine the tofu, broth, yogurt, cashews, mashed potato, vinegar, lemon juice, miso, nutritional yeast (or vegan parmesan), pepper, and 1 teaspoon of salt and blend until completely smooth and creamy, stopping to scrape down the sides as needed. It will seem too thick at first, but keep blending. It should turn silky smooth and pourable, with no bits of nuts or potato remaining.

recipe continues »

5. Stir all that cheesy sauce from the blender into the pasta, making sure to scrape it all out. Stir until the pasta is well coated. Taste and add more salt if needed (I used a total of 1¼ teaspoons). This amount will depend on how well you salted the pasta water. It should have a nice cheesy, salty bite. You want the flavor to stand out after baking, as it will mellow out, so don't worry if it tastes a tad too salty at this point. I also like to add some black pepper as well.

6. Spoon the mixture into an 8 × 8-inch stoneware baking dish and level off the top.

7. In a small bowl, mix together the panko, paprika, and a pinch of salt in a small bowl. (My panko already contained salt, so I only added a pinch, but the amount you add will vary depending on the kind of panko used.) Spread this mixture evenly over the top of the pasta.

8. Bake for 15 minutes. Then turn the broiler on for 1 to 2 minutes only, watching closely so the top doesn't burn! It should turn golden brown. Remove and serve immediately.

NOTES

- If you don't want to use tofu, you can just sub in some more cashews, using ¾ cup (112g) total cashews and sub a chickpea miso for the soy miso.
- To press tofu: Use a tofu press if you have one. Otherwise, place several layers of paper towel on a large plate or cutting board. Set the tofu on the paper towels and top with more paper towels. Place a weight (like a skillet filled with canned goods) on top to help press the water out of the tofu.
- For even more protein, sub in lentil or chickpea pasta for the wheat pasta, keeping in mind that the flavor and texture will change.
- For the cashews: If you do not have a high-powered blender (such as a Vitamix), you need to soak the cashews in a bowl of water to cover overnight. When ready to cook, drain and process in a food processor (which works better than a weak blender).

NUTRITION: 348.4 CALORIES   18.3g PROTEIN   52.8g CARBS   8.8g FAT   13.4g FIBER   2.6g SUGAR   541.3mg SODIUM

thai green sweet potato curry

This recipe only requires a few ingredients but packs a serious punch of flavor! You may have had red curry many times, but green curry is less expected. And no, green curry paste does not taste the same as red. This curry is unique in flavor, with noticeable ginger notes; and the unexpected topping of asparagus is a lovely addition. It has sweetness, spiciness, and a touch of tang from the fresh lime juice. This curry is also excellent with flatbread for delicious dipping!

12 ounces asparagus, tough ends cut off (see Note)

1 lime wedge, plus 1 tablespoon (15g) fresh lime juice

Fine sea salt and freshly ground black pepper

1½-inch knob fresh ginger (12g), minced

4 cups (520g) ½-inch pieces sweet potatoes (peeled)

1 (13.6-ounce) can unsweetened full-fat coconut milk (I love and suggest Thai Kitchen brand)

4 tablespoons (60g) vegan green curry paste

1½ teaspoons coconut sugar

¼ teaspoon red pepper flakes

2 large handfuls of fresh spinach (75g)

FOR SERVING (OPTIONAL)

Cooked white rice

Chopped cilantro, for garnish

Cashews, toasted (see Note, page 173)

Easy Go-To Flatbread (page 71)

1. Preheat the oven to 425°F. Line a sheet pan with parchment paper.

2. Spread the trimmed asparagus evenly on the lined pan and squeeze just a bit of lime juice over them. Season with salt and pepper to taste.

3. Roast until fork-tender, but still firm, 8 to 9 minutes.

4. Meanwhile, in a large pot, bring ½ cup (120g) water to a simmer over medium heat. Once simmering, add the ginger and sweet potatoes. Cover and cook 8 minutes. This process will kick-start softening the sweet potatoes.

5. While the potatoes are cooking, in a large bowl, whisk together the coconut milk, curry paste, coconut sugar, pepper flakes, and ¼ teaspoon salt until smooth.

recipe continues »

6. Once the 8 minutes for the potatoes are up, add the milk mixture and stir well in the pan. Return to a simmer and cook another 5 minutes or so as needed to thicken it just a bit and ensure the potatoes are tender. You just want to slightly thicken the curry, not cook away all that yummy sauce.

7. Stir in the 1 tablespoon lime juice and heat through about 30 seconds. Remove from the heat. Taste and if needed, add more salt.

8. Add to bowls and serve with rice, if desired. Add the roasted asparagus on top. If desired, garnish with fresh cilantro and toasted cashews. If you want even more heat, add more red pepper flakes.

NOTE While asparagus works beautifully here, if you are not a fan or don't have access to some, any steamed greens like kale or spinach would be lovely as well.

NUTRITION: 436 CALORIES 8g PROTEIN 41.2g CARBS 29.6g FAT 6.9g FIBER 10.8g SUGAR 626.3mg SODIUM

sweet and sour tofu with ramen

I love this recipe for many reasons. It comes together easily and combines two foods I eat often: tofu and ramen. Since I love both foods so much, I wanted to create a delicious sauce different from my others. Sweet and sour is a flavor I've always loved in both soups and sauces before I went vegan, so that was the inspiration here. This dish makes me happy every time I make it! While this recipe can be served right away, the flavors significantly improve overnight, as the pasta and tofu really absorb the sauce and the dish is more bold in flavor. Therefore, I recommend making this the day before you want to serve it, if possible.

10 ounce extra-firm tofu

2 tablespoons (30g) reduced-sodium soy sauce

2 tablespoons (30g) fresh lime juice

2½ tablespoons (50g) agave syrup

3 tablespoons (48g) raw cashew butter (with no added oils/sugar; see Notes)

1 tablespoon (15g) tomato paste

½ teaspoon garlic powder

¾ to 1 teaspoon ground ginger, to taste

¼ teaspoon red pepper flakes, plus more for garnish

Fine sea salt and freshly ground black pepper

1 red bell pepper, sliced into strips (160g)

3 cups (195g) broccoli florets

1 (2 ounce) packet ramen noodles (wheat or gluten-free)

3 tablespoons sliced green onions, for garnish

1 tablespoon toasted sesame seeds, for garnish

Hot sauce (optional)

1. Press the tofu (see Notes) and let sit for about 15 minutes. This step is very important to keep the tofu from tasting bland.

2. Meanwhile, in a medium bowl, combine ½ cup plus 1 tablespoon (135g) water, the soy sauce, lime juice, agave, cashew butter, tomato paste, garlic powder, ginger, and pepper flakes and whisk very well. Set the sauce aside.

3. Slice the tofu into ¼ × 1-inch-thick pieces. Salt and pepper well on both sides and add to a very large nonstick frying pan over medium heat. Cook the tofu until well browned on both sides, about 5 to 10 minutes on the first side and about 5 minutes on the second side.

recipe continues »

4. Remove the tofu from the pan and place it in the bowl of the reserved sauce to sit while cooking the vegetables.

5. Add the bell pepper and a few tablespoons of water to the pan, season with salt and pepper, and cook the bell pepper over medium heat, stirring occasionally, until tender, about 5 minutes.

6. Add the broccoli, cover, and steam until tender but still crisp, about 5 minutes.

7. Meanwhile, heat up the ramen noodles according to the package directions (discard the seasoning packet). If using gluten-free, be careful not to overcook them or they will turn mushy when added to the sauce. Drain the noodles well.

8. Add the tofu and sauce to the pan with the veggies. Add the cooked noodles and toss everything together until everything is well coated with sauce. Serve hot garnished with pepper flakes, green onions, and sesame seeds. These toppings are important to really enhance the overall flavor. If you like it extra spicy, add a drizzle of hot sauce!

NOTES

- To press tofu: Use a tofu press if you have one. Otherwise, place several layers of paper towel on a large plate or cutting board. Set the tofu on the paper towels and top with more paper towels. Place a weight (like a skillet filled with canned goods) on top to help press the water out of the tofu.
- If you are allergic to cashews, you can substitute with tahini or sunflower seed butter, keeping in mind it will change the flavor to be a little bit less sweet.

NUTRITION: 299.3 CALORIES   13.7g PROTEIN   32.1g CARBS   14.2g FAT   4.2g FIBER   12.6g SUGAR   608.3mg SODIUM

guestworthy jackfruit lentil curry

This curry is so meaty, people wouldn't know the jackfruit isn't shredded chicken. It looks and resembles it so much. The curry flavors are out of this world and it has such a hearty texture. Your kitchen will be filled with the best aromas, too. I use the same method for baking the jackfruit first like I did with the Jackfruit Pinto Bean Chili (page 134). It's simply the best way to prepare jackfruit. Make sure you are using jackfruit that comes in water and not the sweet syrup, or the curry will be overly sweet!

1 (14-ounce) can young green jackfruit, drained

¼ cup raw cashews (40g; see Notes) or sunflower seeds (36g)

3½ cups (840g) low-sodium vegetable broth

1 cup (160g) finely chopped white onion

1 cup (145g) ¼-inch-thick slices carrots

5 garlic cloves (17g), minced

2 tablespoons (30g) tomato paste

1 tablespoon curry powder, homemade (see page 259) or store-bought

½ teaspoon garam masala

1 teaspoon fine sea salt

½ cup (115g) red lentils, rinsed

1 tablespoon (20g) maple syrup or agave syrup

FOR SERVING (OPTIONAL)

Cooked rice

Cashews, toasted (see Notes)

Lime wedges

1. Preheat the oven to 375°F. Line a sheet pan with parchment paper.

2. In a bowl, use two forks to shred the drained jackfruit very thoroughly like shredded chicken. I also like to use my hands, which makes the process move quicker. For the tougher chunks, use a knife to slice them.

3. Add the shredded jackfruit to a sieve and place paper towels on top to press and squeeze out extra liquid. The drier the jackfruit, the better the result for a chicken-like texture in the final dish. Spread the jackfruit out on the lined sheet pan evenly.

4. Bake until browned, about 25 minutes, watching closely the last few minutes so it does not burn.

recipe continues »

5. Meanwhile, in a high-powered blender, combine the cashews and ½ cup (120g) water and process until completely smooth and no bits remain. Set aside.

6. In a medium pot, bring ½ cup (120g) of the broth to a simmer over medium heat. Add the onions and cook, stirring occasionally, until translucent, about 5 minutes.

7. Add the carrots, garlic, and another ½ cup (120g) broth, cover, and cook for 5 minutes.

8. Add the tomato paste, curry powder, garam masala, and salt and cook for about 1 minute, stirring constantly, until fragrant. Add the remaining 2½ cups (590g) of broth, the lentils, and maple syrup and stir well. Bring back to a simmer, then reduce the heat to low, partially cover (to allow a small amount of steam to escape), and cook until the lentils reach your desired doneness, about 5 minutes.

9. Add the cooked jackfruit and cashew cream and cook for just a few minutes to heat through.

10. Serve as is or with cooked rice. Garnish with lime wedges and toasted cashews, if desired.

NOTES

- If you do not have a high-powered blender (such as a Vitamix), you need to soak the cashews in a bowl of water to cover overnight. When ready to cook, drain and process in a food processor (which works better than a weak blender).
- To toast cashews, add the desired amount to a small skillet over low heat. Stir often just until they are browned, a couple of minutes, being careful not to burn them.

NUTRITION: 358.4 CALORIES   13g PROTEIN   62.1g CARBS   7.3g FAT   12.1g FIBER   15.8g SUGAR   814.2mg SODIUM

sweet potato curry pasta

I love sweet potatoes so much and usually add them to my curry recipes, so I got an idea to try blending sweet potatoes and making a curry sauce with them. It turned out beyond my expectations. Putting the sauce over pasta is a fun twist that is delicious, simple, and nutritious, and using gluten-free lentil pasta gives a hefty dose of protein.

Fine sea salt

12 ounces lentil pasta

½ cup (120g) mashed cooked sweet potato (see Note, page 225)

1 cup (240g) unsweetened creamy plant-based milk (I used almond)

2 tablespoons (30g) vegan Thai red curry paste

¼ cup (60g) plain tomato sauce/passata

2 tablespoons (30g) fresh lime juice

2 teaspoons (10g) reduced-sodium soy sauce

1 teaspoon pure maple syrup or agave syrup

2 tablespoons (26g) hemp hearts

1 teaspoon yellow curry powder, homemade (see page 259) or store-bought

1 teaspoon minced fresh ginger

¼ teaspoon freshly ground black pepper, plus more to taste

⅛ teaspoon cayenne pepper (omit if serving to kids)

Chiffonade of fresh basil (optional), for garnish

Lime wedges, for squeezing

1. Bring a pot of water to a boil for the pasta. Salt the water well, add the pasta and cook according to the package directions.

2. Meanwhile, in a high-powered blender, combine the mashed sweet potato, milk, curry paste, tomato sauce, lime juice, soy sauce, maple syrup, hemp hearts, curry powder, ginger, black pepper, and cayenne (if using) and blend until completely smooth and creamy. If you have a Vitamix, you can blend until the sauce gets hot. If you don't, briefly heat the sauce in a saucepan until warm to serve with the pasta. Taste and, if needed, add salt.

3. Divide the pasta among 4 bowls. Top each serving with sauce and garnish with basil, if desired. Serve with lime wedges for squeezing and season with salt and pepper to taste before serving.

NUTRITION: 339 CALORIES   20.1g PROTEIN   48.7g CARBS   6.6g FAT   6.5g FIBER   5.8g SUGAR   565mg SODIUM

harissa almond pasta with spinach

This bold-flavored pasta takes just a few minutes to put together and is spicy, creamy, and so delicious for a quick meal! The lentils add extra protein, iron, and body to the sauce and the spinach ups the nutritional benefits. Who knew pasta could be so healthy?!

½ cup (80g) chopped red onion

¾ cup (180g) unsweetened creamy plant-based milk (I used almond)

2 to 3 tablespoons (30g to 45g) harissa, to taste

2 tablespoons (32g) roasted almond butter (with no added oils/sugar, or tahini for nut-free)

1 tablespoon (15g) coconut aminos

1 tablespoon (15g) fresh lime juice, plus more to taste

¼ cup (48g) cooked red lentils, well drained

½ teaspoon garlic powder

Fine sea salt and freshly ground black pepper (optional)

12 ounces pasta of choice, either wheat or gluten-free

4 large handfuls of fresh spinach (150g), cooked (I steamed the spinach)

Red pepper flakes (optional), for garnish

NOTES

- Two tablespoons harissa sauce will give a nice kick of heat, and 3 tablespoons will be quite spicy.
- Use gluten-free lentil pasta for even higher protein. I used regular wheat pasta here.
- For a lower-carb option and extra protein, serve the sauce with my All-Purpose Smoky Tofu (page 277).

1. In a nonstick skillet, cook the onions with a splash of water over medium-low heat, stirring often, until they become caramelized and take on a brown color, 5 to 8 minutes. Add tiny bits of water if needed to prevent burning.

2. In a blender, combine the cooked onions, milk, 2 tablespoons of the harissa, the almond butter, coconut aminos, lime juice, cooked lentils, and garlic powder and blend until completely smooth. Taste and add more harissa if you want it spicier and more lime juice it if you want it tangier. Add salt and/or pepper, if desired.

3. Bring a large pot of water to a boil for the pasta. Salt the water well, add the pasta, and cook according to the package directions. Drain well.

4. Add the pasta to bowls and top with desired amount of sauce and the cooked spinach. Garnish with pepper flakes, if desired.

NUTRITION: 413.4 CALORIES   15.8g PROTEIN   73.1g CARBS   6.4g FAT   7.1g FIBER   4.6g SUGAR   318.3mg SODIUM

swedish meatballs

This recipe was one of the most requested when I asked my readers what they would like to see in this cookbook. It took a couple of trials to nail them, but they turned out hearty and so satisfying. They are packed with protein and healthy carbs and lots of flavor. You can serve them with the Swedish gravy and over mashed potatoes or in a bed of cooked pasta for an extra hearty meal!

½ cup (80g) diced red onion

2 tablespoons (30g) reduced-sodium soy sauce

1 teaspoon garlic powder

1 teaspoon onion powder

½ teaspoon ground allspice

½ teaspoon ground ginger

¼ teaspoon ground nutmeg

¼ teaspoon freshly ground black pepper

½ teaspoon fine sea salt

1 (15-ounce) can lentils, drained and rinsed, or 1½ cups (255g) cooked lentils

½ cup (100g) cooked brown rice

¾ cup (75g) old-fashioned rolled oats (gluten-free if needed)

¼ cup (20g) panko bread crumbs (gluten-free if needed)

Swedish Gravy (page 256)

¼ cup chopped fresh parsley, for garnish

1. Preheat the oven to 375°F. Line a sheet pan with parchment paper.

2. In a food processor, combine the onion, soy sauce, garlic powder, onion powder, allspice, ginger, nutmeg, black pepper, and salt and pulse until briefly mixed. Add the lentils, rice, oats, and panko and pulse until the oats are broken up and the mixture all comes together into a cohesive mixture and holds together when pressed between your fingers. If the mixture is a bit too wet, add more panko crumbs just until it comes together.

3. Divide the mixture into 18 equal portions (I like to use a 1½-tablespoon cookie scoop for even measuring) and roll into balls. Arrange the balls on the lined sheet pan.

4. Bake for 20 minutes on the first side. Carefully flip them and cook until golden brown and firm, another 15 minutes or so.

5. Let the meatballs cool a few minutes and serve with the Swedish gravy and parsley.

NUTRITION (3 meatballs): 332.9 CALORIES   22.5g PROTEIN   57.4g CARBS   2.7g FAT   23g FIBER   4.3g SUGAR   321.7mg SODIUM

bbq jackfruit cheese pizzas

Wow! That's what I said when I took the first bite of this incredible pizza! The combo of barbecue sauce, my homemade mozzarella cheese, and the meaty texture of twice-baked jackfruit was magical in every way. My secret to improving jackfruit's somewhat slimy texture is baking it first to dry it out and then baking it again with the pizza toppings to mimic a shredded chicken texture. This will be a crowd-pleaser for sure! Make sure you are using jackfruit that is in water or lime juice and not the kind that comes in a sugary syrup.

If making homemade mozzarella cheese, barbecue sauce, and/or pizza sauce, have them all made before preparing the pizzas. Both the barbecue sauce and pizza sauce only take about 5 minutes to make. However, to make the pizzas come together quickly for dinner, you can make the cheese and sauces the day before, so they're already on hand for future use.

1 (14-ounce) can young green jackfruit, drained

6 tablespoons (90g) barbecue sauce, homemade (see page 251) or store-bought

¾ cup (180g) pizza sauce, homemade (see page 252) or store-bought

4 flatbreads, homemade (see page 71) or store-bought, or 1 large prebaked pizza crust

1 red bell pepper, roughly chopped

½ cup (70g) pickled jalapeño slices

1 cup (240g) Vegan Mozzarella Cheese (page 268) or store-bought liquid mozzarella (such as Miyoko's)

Red pepper flakes (optional)

Handful of fresh basil leaves, roughly chopped

1. Preheat the oven to 375°F. Line a sheet pan with parchment paper.

2. In a bowl, use two forks to shred the drained jackfruit very thoroughly like shredded chicken. I also like to use my hands to make the process quicker. For the tougher chunks, use a knife to slice them.

3. Add the shredded jackfruit to a sieve and place paper towels on top to press and squeeze out extra liquid. The drier the jackfruit, the better the result for a chicken-like texture on the pizza. Spread the jackfruit out evenly on the sheet pan.

recipe continues »

4. Bake until browned, about 25 minutes, watching closely the last few minutes so it does not burn. Remove the jackfruit but leave the oven on and increase the temperature to 400°F for the pizzas.

5. In a bowl, combine the cooked jackfruit and barbecue sauce and mix well.

6. To assemble the pizzas, spread 3 tablespoons of pizza sauce on each of the 4 flatbreads leaving a slight gap around the edges. Or spread ¾ cup on a large pizza crust.

7. Divide the baked jackfruit onto the pizzas, adding as much as you desire. Add the bell pepper and jalapeños. Add spoonfuls of the mozzarella cheese on each pizza and top with red pepper flakes, if desired. Don't add the basil until after the pizzas are baked.

8. Bake the flatbread pizzas until the cheese is firm, about 10 minutes (this time can vary if you use store-bought cheese). If using a large pizza crust, bake 10 to 15 minutes. Top with fresh basil and serve immediately.

NUTRITION (1 flatbread): 463.5 CALORIES   13.2g PROTEIN   94.7g CARBS   11.5g FAT   10.3g FIBER   15.1g SUGAR   1264.6mg SODIUM

cheesy quinoa
poblano peppers

These are not only pretty to look at, but they pack a punch of nutrition and flavor. The spices, fluffy quinoa, and my amazing mozzarella all combine to make one delicious meal to impress your guests! If you are wanting more fat than just the cheese, avocado slices on top are good, too!

3 large poblano peppers, sliced in half lengthwise, seeds and membranes removed

½ cup (94g) quinoa, rinsed well

½ teaspoon chili powder

½ teaspoon garlic powder

½ teaspoon ground cumin

¼ teaspoon fine sea salt, plus more to taste

1 cup (170g) cooked black beans, drained

½ cup (85g) frozen sweet corn kernels

1 tablespoon (15g) fresh lime juice, plus more for serving

Freshly ground black pepper

½ cup (120g) liquid vegan mozzarella, homemade (see page 268) or store-bought (such as Miyoko's; see Note)

Red pepper flakes

1. Preheat the oven to 350°F. Line a sheet pan with parchment paper.

2. Arrange the poblano pepper halves cut-side up on the lined sheet pan. Bake for 15 minutes and remove from oven. Leave the oven on and increase the temperature to 400°F.

3. Meanwhile, in a medium pot, combine the quinoa, 1 cup (240g) water, the chili powder, garlic powder, cumin, and salt and stir well. Bring to a boil. Reduce the heat to low, cover, and simmer 15 minutes. Remove from the heat and let sit covered for 5 minutes. Fluff the quinoa with a fork.

4. In a large bowl, add 1 cup (180g) of the cooked quinoa (you'll have some quinoa left over), the beans, corn, and lime juice. Stir well. Taste and add more salt and any pepper if needed.

5. Fill each pepper with the quinoa mixture carefully, using all the mixture. The top of the quinoa mixture will be higher than the peppers. Drizzle the mozzarella cheese over the tops of each pepper. Top with red pepper flakes to taste.

recipe continues »

6. Return to the oven and bake until the cheese is firmed up and golden on the tips, about 10 minutes. The peppers should be perfectly tender by this point. I like to turn the broiler on for just a minute at the end to give the cheese a more golden brown color, but this is only for aesthetic reasons. If using store-bought cheese, the broiler is not necessary.

7. Serve hot. An extra squeeze of lime juice is nice right at serving, too.

NOTE   You can substitute a shredded vegan mozzarella for the liquid vegan mozzarella. Use ½ cup (56g) of the shredded mozzarella and follow the recipe as directed.

NUTRITION (1 half pepper): 148.3 CALORIES   6.4g PROTEIN   25.1g CARBS   3.1g FAT   4.8g FIBER   2.1g SUGAR   153.8mg SODIUM

teriyaki stuffed bell peppers

I'm a little obsessed with teriyaki sauce, and for good reason, because it works well with so many types of recipes. I love my homemade teriyaki sauce so much better than store-bought because the flavor is stronger and not as high in sodium. Plus, it takes less than 10 minutes to make. It also takes these grains and veggies up a serious notch, and provides a great flavor to pair with the roasted sweetness of the bell peppers.

3 red bell peppers, halved and seeded

1 cup (160g) finely chopped white onion

3 large garlic cloves (11g), minced

1 teaspoon minced fresh ginger

2 cups (170g) broccoli florets

1 cup (145g) cooked quinoa or brown rice

½ cup (85g) cooked green peas (or shelled edamame for higher protein)

½ cup (120g) teriyaki sauce, homemade (see page 248) or store-bought, plus more (optional) for drizzling

1 tablespoon (10g) toasted sesame seeds, for garnish

¼ cup sliced green onions, for garnish

1. Preheat the oven to 375°F.

2. Place the bell peppers in a baking dish and set aside.

3. In a large pan, bring ½ cup (120g) water to a simmer over medium heat. Add the onion and cook until translucent, about 5 minutes. Add the garlic and ginger and cook another couple of minutes, until tender. Add the broccoli, cover, and steam until fork-tender, but not mushy, just a few minutes. Remove from the heat.

4. In a large bowl, combine the cooked veggie mixture, quinoa, peas, and teriyaki sauce and toss to coat everything well.

5. Spoon this mixture evenly into each halved bell pepper, piling it up carefully. Cover the baking dish with foil.

6. Bake for 20 minutes. Remove the foil and bake until the bell peppers are tender to your liking, another 10 to 20 minutes.

7. Serve garnished with the sesame seeds, green onions, and another drizzle of teriyaki sauce, if desired.

NUTRITION (1 half pepper): 181.2 CALORIES   7g PROTEIN   34g CARBS   2.7g FAT   5.2g FIBER   10.2g SUGAR   257.2mg SODIUM

cajun spinach artichoke pasta

I love a kick of heat for dinner and anything Cajun fits the bill. Most of us know and love the classic spinach and artichoke dip that is often served at parties. I even have that dip in my first cookbook. But I wanted something unique and unexpected, so I expanded that classic by adding a Cajun flare and also transforming it into a pasta dish. If you want higher protein, make sure to use a pasta like lentil or chickpea.

Fine sea salt

1 cup (112g) uncooked red lentil fusilli pasta or wheat pasta

½ cup raw cashews (75g; see Note) or sunflower seeds (56g)

2 cups (480g) low-sodium vegetable broth

2 tablespoons (16g) nutritional yeast

2 teaspoons red miso paste

2 teaspoons fresh lemon juice

3½ teaspoons Cajun Seasoning (page 264)

1 (14-ounce) can artichoke hearts, water-packed and drained

1 tablespoon (15g) capers

3 handfuls of fresh spinach (70g)

NOTE If you do not have a high-powered blender (such as a Vitamix), you need to soak the cashews in a bowl of water to cover overnight. When ready to cook, drain and process in a food processor (which works better than a weak blender).

1. Bring a small pot of water to a boil for the pasta. Salt the water well, add the pasta and cook according to the package directions, but just under al dente. Drain and set aside.

2. Meanwhile, in a high-powered blender, combine the cashews, broth, nutritional yeast, miso, lemon juice, and Cajun seasoning and blend until completely smooth and no bits of nuts remain.

3. In a large saucepan, combine the blended sauce, cooked pasta, artichokes, and capers and bring to a simmer over medium heat. Cook, stirring occasionally, until the sauce thickens to your desired consistency, 5 to 10 minutes. It will seem really runny at first, but it will thicken beautifully after several minutes.

4. Once it's almost as thick as you'd like, stir in the spinach and heat through just until wilted. Taste and add more salt, if needed. If you would like it more spicy, add a bit more Cajun seasoning. Serve immediately.

NUTRITION: 423.6 CALORIES   20.9g PROTEIN   64.7g CARBS   12.2g FAT   18.9g FIBER   7.3g SUGAR   817.4mg SODIUM

sweet and savory snacks

Supremely Rich Brownie Protein Bites ——————— 193

Pistachio Chocolate Cups ——————— 194

Apple Pie Spice Balls ——————— 197

Mocha Chocolate Chip Granola ——————— 198

Seedy Coconut Trail Mix ——————— 201

Protein-Rich BBQ Sesame Tofu Bites ——————— 202

Smoky Bean Dip ——————— 205

My Favorite Oil-Free Hummus ——————— 206

Pizza Chickpea Balls ——————— 209

Baked Zucchini Crisps ——————— 210

supremely rich brownie protein bites

If you love brownies, but also want a good dose of protein, these decadent bites are for you! These are very rich, dense, and only for serious chocolate lovers. I use the Sprout Living Epic Protein Chocolate Maca protein powder for my recipes. It is the best! This powder is sweetened, so keep that in mind when you choose a protein powder—and also be sure that you love the taste, since this uses quite a lot of it.

4 scoops (64g) vegan chocolate protein powder

6 tablespoons (36g) unsweetened cocoa powder

¼ teaspoon fine sea salt

¼ cup (60g) unsweetened plant-based milk

¼ cup (80g) maple syrup or agave syrup

¼ cup (64g) raw cashew butter (with no added oils/sugar)

¼ cup (60g) dairy-free semisweet chocolate chips

1. In a medium bowl, whisk together the protein powder, cocoa powder, and salt. Add the milk, maple syrup, cashew butter, and chocolate chips. Stir until it comes together into a thick, sticky ball. Use your hands if needed to form a thick dough.

2. Divide the dough into 16 equal portions, using a cookie scoop. Roll them into about 1-inch balls with your hands. You can eat them right away or place them in the fridge to chill first. Store any leftovers at room temperature or in the fridge, covered, so they don't dry out. I love them cold straight from the fridge. You can even store them in the freezer so they last longer, but allow them to thaw a bit first before eating. They will keep for 2 weeks in the fridge and a couple of months in the freezer.

NUTRITION (2 bites): 153.1 CALORIES   8g PROTEIN   17.5g CARBS   7.7g FAT   2.5g FIBER   9.9g SUGAR   134.5mg SODIUM

pistachio chocolate cups

Pistachios are by far my favorite nuts, and when you combine their buttery taste with chocolate, it's a winning combo! These cups have an addicting texture and flavor, making them the perfect sweet snack to munch on and satisfy hunger quickly.

1 cup (100g) old-fashioned rolled oats (gluten-free if needed)

½ cup (80g) pistachios, plus more (optional) for garnish

½ teaspoon ground cinnamon

¼ teaspoon fine sea salt

3 tablespoons (48g) raw cashew butter (with no added oils/sugar)

¼ cup (80g) pure maple syrup or agave syrup

½ teaspoon vanilla extract

½ cup (120g) dairy-free semisweet chocolate chips (see Note)

1 tablespoon (15g) unsweetened almond milk or other plant-based milk

NOTES

- Using all semisweet chocolate chips will make this a fairly sweet dessert, which is what I prefer. If you don't like things too sweet, I'd suggest doing half semisweet and half bittersweet chocolate chips.
- These cups will keep for 2 weeks in the fridge and a couple of months in the freezer.

1. In a food processor, process the oats until they are a fine flour consistency. Add the pistachios, cinnamon, and salt and blend until the pistachios are in tiny pieces, but not as fine as flour. Add the cashew butter, maple syrup, vanilla, and ¼ cup (60g) of the chocolate chips and process until a thick, cohesive, and sticky ball comes together. The mixture should hold together when pressed between your fingers.

2. Line 8 cups of a muffin tin with paper liners. Divide the dough among the cups (about the size of a golf ball for each) and press the mixture down firmly until flat and even with your fingers. Use the back of a spoon to even out the tops and press down further.

3. In a small microwave-safe bowl, combine the remaining ¼ cup (60g) of chocolate chips and the milk. Microwave in 10-second increments, stirring well after each, until completely melted, 20 to 30 seconds. Be very careful about overheating the chocolate or it will burn.

4. Spoon the melted chocolate over each pistachio cup and spread it out. These can be topped with a few extra pistachios for a pretty presentation at this stage, if desired. Place the muffin pan in the fridge for several minutes until the chocolate sets. I then store them at room temperature because I preferred the texture. However, if you like them on the firmer side, store in the fridge.

NUTRITION (1 pistachio cup): 246 CALORIES   5.7g PROTEIN   28.7g CARBS   13.3g FAT   3.5g FIBER   14g SUGAR   64.8mg SODIUM

apple pie spice balls

These easy-to-make snack balls have the delicious flavors of apple pie, but without all the work. While I love the balls plain, I decided to crush graham crackers to coat them. Since graham crackers are a common choice for pie crusts, this really drove home the apple pie flavor! These were also a huge hit with my daughter, Olivia.

¼ cup (64g) raw cashew butter (with no added oils/sugar)

2 tablespoons (32g) almond butter (with no added oils/sugar)

2 tablespoons (30g) unsweetened applesauce

¼ cup (80g) pure maple syrup or agave syrup

1½ teaspoons ground cinnamon

½ teaspoon ground allspice

½ teaspoon ground nutmeg

1 tablespoon (8g) coconut sugar

Pinch of fine sea salt

1 cup (100g) quick-cooking oats (gluten-free if needed)

¼ cup (32g) oat flour (gluten-free if needed)

2 vegan graham crackers, crushed (see Note)

1. In a large bowl, whisk together the cashew butter, almond butter, applesauce, maple syrup, cinnamon, allspice, nutmeg, coconut sugar, and salt. Add the oats and oat flour and stir until a very thick dough forms, using the back of a spoon to press the mixture together.

2. Divide the mixture into 12 equal portions using a cookie scoop, then roll them into tight balls with the palms of your hands.

3. On a small plate, spread out the graham cracker crumbs. Roll each ball in the crumbs until evenly coated. Set onto a separate plate or container and refrigerate for 1 to 2 hours to firm up a bit and make them easier to eat. After that you can either store them at room temperature or in the fridge. I like them in the fridge.

NOTE   You can crush the graham crackers by hand or add them to a zip-seal bag and pound them until crushed.

NUTRITION (1 ball): 117.4 CALORIES   3.1g PROTEIN   16.1g CARBS   5.1g FAT   1.7g FIBER   5.5g SUGAR   34.3mg SODIUM

mocha chocolate chip granola

This is by far my favorite granola! To me, there is no better combo than chocolate and coffee. Add some molasses for extra depth of flavor and you have a robust, knock-your-socks-off granola that will beat any version you can buy from the store. I store this granola in on-the-go containers for snacks. I love to eat it plain because it is so addicting. But if you'd like to serve it as a dessert, then use it to make parfaits. Simply add some granola to a small glass, add some vegan yogurt of your choice and top with raspberries.

3 cups (300g) old-fashioned rolled oats (gluten-free if needed)

5 tablespoons (30g) unsweetened cocoa powder

2 tablespoons (8g) instant coffee grounds

¼ teaspoon fine sea salt

⅓ cup (50g) finely chopped pistachios or any desired nut

¼ cup (60g) dairy-free mini semisweet chocolate chips

½ cup (160g) pure maple syrup or agave syrup

2 tablespoons (40g) regular molasses (not blackstrap)

¼ cup (64g) runny almond butter (with no added oils/sugar)

1 teaspoon vanilla extract

NOTE To make this nut-free, omit the pistachios or use a seed of choice and sub in sunflower seed butter or tahini for the almond butter if you don't mind the stronger taste.

1. Preheat the oven to 325°F. Line a large sheet pan with parchment paper.

2. In a large bowl, combine the oats, cocoa powder, coffee grounds, salt, and pistachios and stir well. Stir in the chocolate chips.

3. In a medium bowl, combine the maple syrup, molasses, almond butter, and vanilla and whisk well until smooth. Pour the liquids over the dry ingredients and stir for several minutes until the mixture is evenly damp. Spread the mixture over the lined pan into a flat layer.

4. Bake for 15 minutes. Stir the granola around so the underside can cook. Return to the oven and bake for another 15 minutes.

5. Let the granola cool on the pan for about 20 minutes or so. It will crisp up as it cools. Store in a glass container for up to 2 weeks.

NUTRITION (½ cup): 276.8 CALORIES 7.3g PROTEIN 42.6g CARBS 10.2g FAT 5.5g FIBER 16.7g SUGAR 69.1mg SODIUM

seedy coconut trail mix

When I tell you how unbelievably scrumptious this trail mix is, I am not exaggerating one bit. One bite into this crunchy heaven, I knew I had created a winner. I'm not even that big of a coconut fan, but when coconut is roasted it becomes so nutty and robust in flavor. When paired with the seeds and the sweetness of the maple syrup and cherries, it is pure magic. This is a high-fat snack containing lots of heathy omega-3 fatty acids, so a couple of handfuls of this during a busy day will completely satisfy any hunger in between meals.

1 cup (85g) unsweetened coconut flakes

¼ cup (45g) pumpkin seeds

3 tablespoons (30g) hemp hearts

2 tablespoons (16g) ground flaxseeds (I used golden)

¼ cup (40g) dried cherries

⅛ teaspoon fine sea salt

3 tablespoons (60g) pure maple syrup

¼ cup (60g) unsweetened applesauce

1. Position a rack in the center of the oven and preheat the oven to 325°F. Line a sheet pan with parchment paper.

2. In a large bowl, stir together the coconut, pumpkin seeds, hemp hearts, ground flaxseeds, cherries, and salt.

3. Pour the syrup and applesauce over the dry ingredients and stir for a few minutes until the mixture is evenly coated and moist. Transfer the mixture to the lined pan and spread it out evenly into a flat layer.

4. Bake for 15 minutes. Stir the trail mix around very well so it bakes evenly throughout. You will notice that the edges have started turning golden brown. Stir those bits toward the center. Flatten the mixture back out and bake until a nice beautiful golden brown, another 10 minutes, watching closely the last couple of minutes so it doesn't burn. Coconut can quickly go from golden brown to burnt, so don't overbake.

5. Let the trail mix cool on the pan for 15 minutes. It will crisp up beautifully as it cools. Store in a sealed container at room temperature for a few days or 2 weeks in the fridge.

NUTRITION (½ cup): 239.9 CALORIES   5.4g PROTEIN   19g CARBS   16.7g FAT   3.5g FIBER   12.7g SUGAR   3.5mg SODIUM

protein-rich bbq sesame tofu bites

What is better than a snack that is high in protein, full of flavor, and easy to make? I fell in love with these tofu bites. The texture and bold flavor make them addictive. While they work great as a snack, they can totally be used in a meal as well. Just pair them with a grain like rice or even pasta and your favorite veggie. The nutty flavor of the sesame works so well with the barbecue sauce and also gives a nice little crunch.

14 ounces extra-firm tofu

2 tablespoons (16g) cornstarch

6 to 8 tablespoons (90g to 120g) Texas-style barbecue sauce, homemade (see page 251) or store-bought

1 tablespoon (8g) sesame seeds

1 tablespoon chopped fresh parsley (optional)

NOTE   To press tofu: Use a tofu press if you have one. Otherwise, place several layers of paper towel on a large plate or cutting board. Set the tofu on the paper towels and top with more paper towels. Place a weight (like a skillet filled with canned goods) on top to help press the water out of the tofu.

1.   Preheat the oven to 425°F. Line a sheet pan with parchment paper.

2.   Press the tofu (see Note) and let sit for about 15 minutes. This is important so that the tofu gets crispy.

3.   Break the tofu into bite-size pieces that are similar in size. Place them in a large bowl. Add the cornstarch and use your hands to gently toss the tofu pieces around so that they are well coated. Be gentle so the tofu bites don't fall apart too much. Spread the pieces out onto the lined pan, leaving space around each piece.

4.   Bake until they are firm, crispy, and a golden color, 30 to 35 minutes.

5.   Add the baked tofu to another bowl and add the 6 tablespoons (90g) of the barbecue sauce. Depending on the consistency of the barbecue sauce, you may need up to 8 tablespoons, as some sauces are thicker than others and you want the tofu fully coated. Add the sesame seeds and stir the tofu around until well coated with the sauce. Add the parsley (if using) and serve immediately.

NUTRITION: 329.2 CALORIES   21.3g PROTEIN   31.4g CARBS   13.1g FAT   3.6g FIBER   15.8g SUGAR   473.7mg SODIUM

smoky bean dip

This dip is straight-up addictive. It is smoky, creamy, full of so much flavor, and it will become a staple in your diet. You can't go wrong with this dip, packed with good-for-you ingredients and healthy carbs and protein. I love to eat this as a snack with either fresh veggies or chips, or even as a spread on toast.

1 (15-ounce) can low-sodium black beans, drained and rinsed, or 1½ cups (255g) cooked beans

1 (15-ounce) can low-sodium pinto beans, drained and rinsed, or 1½ cups (255g) cooked beans

½ heaping cup (80g) finely chopped red bell pepper

½ cup (80g) finely chopped white onion

1 extra-large or 2 medium garlic cloves, minced

2 tablespoons (30g) fresh lime juice

1¼ to 1½ teaspoons ground cumin, to taste

1 teaspoon fine sea salt, plus more to taste

½ teaspoon freshly ground black pepper

½ to 1 teaspoon liquid smoke, to taste

1 to 2 tablespoons finely chopped fresh jalapeño, to taste

Chopped jalapeño and red bell pepper, for garnish

Lime wedges, for squeezing

NOTES

- If you would like to eat this dip more as a meal and include some fat, add sliced avocado. It's also delicious on toast or in tortilla roll-ups.
- I recommend making it and refrigerating a few hours or making it the day before serving.

1. Pour the beans into a food processor.

2. In a small nonstick frying pan, combine the bell pepper, onion, and 3 tablespoons (45g) water and cook over medium-low heat, stirring a bit, until tender, for about 5 minutes. Add the garlic and cook a couple of minutes more. Everything should be softened by about 8 minutes. If necessary, add a tiny bit more water to keep it cooking, but make sure all the water is completely gone before adding it to the beans.

3. Add the cooked veggies, lime juice, cumin, salt, black pepper, and liquid smoke to the beans in the processor and process until smooth, scraping the sides a couple of times as needed. Add the chopped jalapeño and process just a few seconds more until blended in (I used a heaping tablespoon, but if you are sensitive, start out with less and add more until you reach the desired heat level). Taste and add more salt, if needed (this can vary based on how salty the beans are). Refrigerate for a few hours.

4. Once ready to serve, garnish with chopped jalapeño and bell pepper (for crunch) and lime wedges for squeezing.

NUTRITION (½ cup): 129.2 CALORIES   8g PROTEIN   24g CARBS   0.7g FAT   8.1g FIBER   1.4g SUGAR   326.1mg SODIUM

my favorite oil-free hummus

I've created a lot of hummus recipes over the years and I love them all. I've also eaten a ton of hummus in my life, especially in restaurants, but they tend to be full of added oil. However, I've never created just a classic basic hummus. This version is so creamy and satisfying without any added oil. The natural oils in the tahini make it creamy enough on its own. For my version, I add a couple of unexpected ingredients you don't typically see in hummus, but it makes it extra flavorful, so just trust me! I love eating hummus as a snack because it's nutritious, full of fiber, healthy carbs, and protein, while also being filling. I like it with a piece of flatbread or with fresh veggies.

1 (15-ounce) can low-sodium chickpeas, drained and rinsed, or 1½ cups (255g) cooked chickpeas

2 tablespoons (30g) fresh lemon juice

3 tablespoons (48g) good-quality smooth tahini (see Note)

2 large garlic cloves (8g), peeled but whole

1 tablespoon (8g) nutritional yeast

1 tablespoon (15g) capers with brine

½ teaspoon smoked paprika

¼ teaspoon ground cumin, optional

½ to ¾ teaspoon fine sea salt, to taste

FOR SERVING (OPTIONAL)

Flatbread, homemade (see page 71) or store-bought

Fresh vegetables

Red pepper flakes and chopped fresh parsley, for garnish

NOTE Make sure you are using a good-quality smooth and runny tahini and not one of those chunky, dry ones. It should be very runny and pour easily. This will make a huge difference in the flavor and texture of the recipe. I love both the Soom brand and the Prince brand.

1. In a food processor, combine the chickpeas, ¼ cup (60g) cold water, the lemon juice, tahini, garlic, nutritional yeast, capers, smoked paprika, cumin, and ½ teaspoon of the salt and blend for at least 5 minutes, stopping to scrape down the sides once or twice in the beginning. Just let it run for several minutes, which will turn it from chunky and gritty to velvety smooth and creamy, dreamy hummus! Taste and add more salt, if needed (this will vary depending on the sodium level of your chickpeas).

2. Serve with flatbread or fresh veggies, if desired, and garnish with pepper flakes and parsley.

NUTRITION (½ cup): 190.4 CALORIES   9g PROTEIN   22.1g CARBS   8.3g FAT   6.6g FIBER   3.4g SUGAR   352.2mg SODIUM

pizza chickpea balls

If you love pizza and meatballs, then you're going to love these! These hearty chickpea balls have the most incredible pizza flavor in every bite. I literally could not get over how delicious they were after I tasted the first one. Dipping them in my easy pizza sauce takes them to the next level.

¼ cup (26g) dry-pack sun-dried tomatoes (not oil-packed)

¾ cup (180g) plain tomato sauce/passata

2 tablespoons (30g) coconut aminos

¼ cup (38g) finely chopped black olives

2 teaspoons salt-free Italian seasoning

3 tablespoons (24g) nutritional yeast

½ teaspoon garlic powder

¼ to ½ teaspoon red pepper flakes, to taste

¼ teaspoon fine sea salt

1 (15-ounce) can low-sodium chickpeas, drained and rinsed, or 1½ cups (255g) cooked chickpeas

½ cup (100g) cooked rice

¾ cup (52g) panko breadcrumbs (gluten-free if needed)

Handful of fresh basil leaves (8g), plus more (optional) for garnish

Easiest Ever Pizza Sauce (page 252; optional), for serving

1. Soak the sun-dried tomatoes in a bowl of hot water for 30 minutes to soften.

2. Preheat the oven to 350°F. Line a sheet pan with parchment paper.

3. Drain the sun-dried tomatoes and add to a food processor. Process a few times, then add the tomato sauce, coconut aminos, olives, Italian seasoning, nutritional yeast, garlic powder, pepper flakes, and salt and briefly pulse just to combine the ingredients.

4. Add the chickpeas, rice, panko, and basil and pulse until it all comes together into one cohesive, sticky mixture. It should hold together when pressed between your fingers.

5. Divide the mixture into 24 equal portions (about 2 tablespoons), using a cookie scoop. With your hands, roll into balls (about the size of a golf ball). Arrange the balls on the lined pan spaced apart.

6. Bake the first side for 25 minutes. Try to carefully flip one and if it sticks to the paper, cook a few more minutes before flipping. Flip and cook until golden brown, about 15 more minutes.

7. Serve with the pizza sauce for dipping and garnish with basil, if desired.

NUTRITION (4 balls): 165 CALORIES   8.3g PROTEIN   28.7g CARBS   2.2g FAT   5.7g FIBER   6.1g SUGAR   311.4mg SODIUM

baked zucchini crisps

Zucchini is easily one of my favorite vegetables. The possibilities are endless with this amazing vegetable. Since I try not to use oil but love fried zucchini chips, I wanted to re-create them without the frying. These use lemon juice and some spices and a coating to give them a wonderful texture on the outside. They are so delicious and will become a favorite healthy snack to munch on! They would even be great as a side veggie at dinner.

¼ cup (20g) panko bread crumbs (use gluten-free if needed)

¼ cup (28g) blanched almond flour

1 tablespoon (10g) cornmeal

1 teaspoon garlic powder

1 teaspoon onion powder

¾ teaspoon fine sea salt

¼ teaspoon freshly ground black pepper

2 large zucchini (300g), cut into ¼-inch-thick rounds

1 tablespoon (15g) fresh lemon juice

Fresh parsley (optional), for garnish

1. Preheat the oven to 425°F. Line a sheet pan with parchment paper.

2. In a large bowl, stir together the panko, almond flour, cornmeal, garlic powder, onion powder, salt, and pepper really well. Set the coating aside.

3. Add the sliced zucchini to a separate medium bowl. Squeeze the lemon juice over the zucchini and toss really well with your hands to make sure all the zucchini is well coated.

4. Place the zucchini slices one by one in the coating mixture, flipping a couple of times, pressing them to make sure they are coated very well and arrange in a single layer on the lined pan.

5. Bake for 20 minutes. Flip them over carefully and bake until browned and slightly crispy on the second side, another 10 minutes or so.

6. These are best served immediately, garnished with parsley, if using. They aren't crispy like chips, but have a slight crispy texture and will soften as they cool.

NUTRITION: 114.4 CALORIES   4.4g PROTEIN   14.2g CARBS   5.1g FAT   2.8g FIBER   3.3g SUGAR   602.4mg SODIUM

CHAPTER 8

feel-good desserts

Almond Cream Strawberry Shortcakes _____ 215

Chocolate Tahini Cookies _____ 217

Chocolate Pots de Crème _____ 220

Sweet Potato Cake _____ 223

Vanilla Protein Mug Cake _____ 226

Mint Chocolate Chip Protein Shake _____ 229

Dark Chocolate Orange-Glazed Scones _____ 230

Sweet Potato Caramel _____ 233

Frozen Strawberry Yogurt Bark with Dark Chocolate _____ 234

Strawberry Orange Sorbet _____ 237

4-Ingredient Peanut Butter Cookies _____ 238

almond cream strawberry shortcakes

I cracked the magical code for the most luscious shortcakes ever. While traditional recipes call for lots of butter and sugar, my recipe uses homemade almond cream. These shortcakes are so moist and rich, and unbelievably creamy! Seriously, I was blown away by the result. If you don't have a scale, I recommend purchasing one; it is a wise investment for baking so the results turn out perfectly. It's too easy to incorrectly measure dry ingredients when using measuring cups. For the vegan whipped cream, I love the classic taste, so I buy the canned spray kind by Reddi-wip. They make a coconut and an almond one. Both are delicious and don't taste strongly of nuts at all. If you don't mind a strong coconut flavor, So Delicious makes a coconut whipped topping (like Cool Whip) sold in the frozen section. You can also totally skip this if you want to avoid the extra sugar.

¾ cup (105g) slivered almonds (see Note)

3 tablespoons (60g) pure maple syrup

1 teaspoon (5g) apple cider vinegar

2 cups (256g) all-purpose flour, plus more for dusting

2¾ teaspoons baking powder

¼ teaspoon baking soda

½ teaspoon fine sea salt

1 cup (166g) sliced fresh strawberries

Vegan whipped cream (optional)

Shaved chocolate (optional), for garnish

1. Preheat the oven to 400°F. Line a sheet pan with parchment paper.

2. In a high-powered blender, combine the almonds and ¾ cup (180g) water and blend on high for about 1 minute until completely smooth and no bits of nuts remain. The texture will be grainy now but will be magical in the final baked result.

3. Add the maple syrup and vinegar to the blender and just briefly blend.

4. In a large bowl, whisk together the flour, baking powder, baking soda, and salt. Pour the almond cream mixture over the dry ingredients, making sure to scrape out the blender well. Stir gently

recipe continues »

until it resembles a rough, lumpy, and sticky dough and no loose flour remains. Avoid overmixing at this point.

5. Lightly flour a work surface and scrape the dough out onto the surface. Using very lightly floured hands, pat the dough into a disc about 7 inches across and ¾ to 1 inch thick. Do not pat down less than ¾ inch or the biscuits will be too short. Be gentle with the dough.

6. Using a 2¾-inch biscuit cutter, press down into the dough and lift up. You should get 4 biscuits the first time. Piece the excess dough together back into a ball and gently pat it back down to ¾ to 1 inch to get 3 to 4 more biscuits. Place the biscuits on the lined pan, just touching each other.

7. Bake until well risen and golden on top, about 13 minutes.

8. Cool 5 to 10 minutes on the pan before serving.

9. To serve, slice each biscuit horizontally in half. Layer with strawberries and whipped cream (if using). Shaved chocolate makes a nice presentation, as well.

NOTE   If you don't have a high-powered blender (like a Vitamix), soak the almonds in boiling water for a couple of hours. Drain and process in a food processor (which works better than a weak blender).

NUTRITION (1 shortcake): 219.6 CALORIES   6.2g PROTEIN   34.3g CARBS   6.9g FAT   2.9g FIBER   6.2g SUGAR   315.5mg SODIUM

chocolate tahini cookies

If you love tahini, then these cookies are for you! These chocolate beauties took four trials to perfect. I wanted them to be super moist, and rich with a lovely balance of chocolate and tahini flavor. Not too sweet and not too bitter was a challenge at first to get the perfect taste, but we have a winner! My daughter helped me by being the judge for each batch, providing perfect feedback until we both fell in love by the fourth trial. These are so decadent, nobody would believe they are vegan, let alone gluten-free, with no nuts or added oil or butter!

½ cup (64g) superfine oat flour (gluten-free if needed)

¼ cup (28g) superfine blanched almond flour

¼ cup (32g) tapioca starch

6 tablespoons (36g) unsweetened cocoa powder

1 teaspoon baking soda

½ teaspoon fine sea salt

¾ cup (192g) good-quality smooth tahini (see Note)

½ cup plus 2 tablespoons (200g) pure maple syrup or agave syrup

1 teaspoon vanilla extract

½ cup (120g) dairy-free semisweet chocolate chips

1. Preheat the oven to 375°F. Line a dark sheet pan with parchment paper. If you only have a light pan, then you may need to bake the cookies 1 minute longer. Additionally, the bottoms won't get as crispy.

2. In a large bowl, whisk together the oat flour, almond flour, tapioca starch, cocoa powder, baking soda, and salt, whisking well to break up any lumps.

3. In a medium bowl, stir together the tahini, maple syrup, and vanilla until smooth. Pour into the dry ingredients and add the chocolate chips. Stir the ingredients together until a moist, thick batter forms. The batter will be thicker than a muffin batter, but not thick enough to roll into balls. Basically, a soft batter that will spread nicely in the oven.

4. Use a 1½-tablespoon cookie scoop and drop spoonfuls of the cookie dough onto the lined pan, spacing them 2 inches apart. Do not flatten out the dough. They will spread out a lot on their own during baking.

recipe continues »

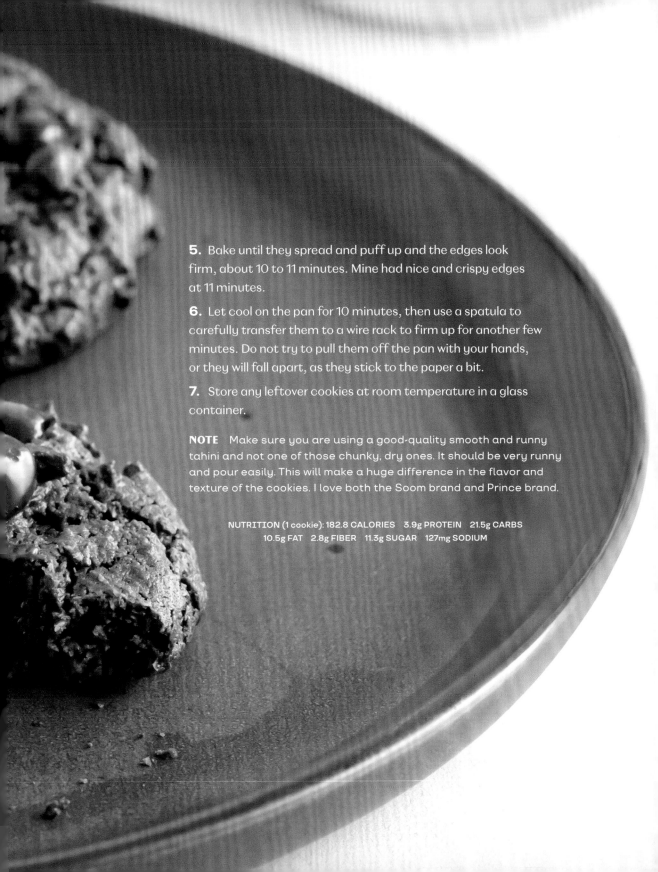

5. Bake until they spread and puff up and the edges look firm, about 10 to 11 minutes. Mine had nice and crispy edges at 11 minutes.

6. Let cool on the pan for 10 minutes, then use a spatula to carefully transfer them to a wire rack to firm up for another few minutes. Do not try to pull them off the pan with your hands, or they will fall apart, as they stick to the paper a bit.

7. Store any leftover cookies at room temperature in a glass container.

NOTE   Make sure you are using a good-quality smooth and runny tahini and not one of those chunky, dry ones. It should be very runny and pour easily. This will make a huge difference in the flavor and texture of the cookies. I love both the Soom brand and Prince brand.

NUTRITION (1 cookie): 182.8 CALORIES   3.9g PROTEIN   21.5g CARBS   10.5g FAT   2.8g FIBER   11.3g SUGAR   127mg SODIUM

chocolate pots de crème

Get ready to be blown away by the dreamiest dessert. These beauties are smooth, creamy, decadent, and rich. Pots de crème are a classic French custard dessert traditionally made with heavy cream and eggs, but I've created a rich vegan version that you and your family will absolutely love. I use cashew butter instead of cream and eggs. Cashew butter works perfectly here because it's high in fat and is naturally sweet, so it blends right into the chocolate, leaving no nutty taste behind. Make sure to use a raw cashew butter without added oil, or it will not set properly. Cashew butter also has less oil than other nut butters (such as almond butter), so I highly recommend not substituting out the cashew butter. If you are allergic, you can use sunflower seed butter, but just keep in mind that the dessert will be more bitter. Make sure you are using "lite" coconut milk and not full-fat, so it will set properly and not leave behind a coconut taste.

½ cup (120g) canned unsweetened "lite" coconut milk or another higher fat creamy milk

½ cup (120g) unsweetened almond milk or other plant-based milk (but not soy milk, which will firm up too much)

¾ cup (150g) dairy-free semisweet chocolate chips

¼ cup (50g) dairy-free bittersweet chocolate chips (69% to 70% cacao)

¼ cup (64g) raw cashew butter (with no added oils/sugar)

1 tablespoon (20g) maple syrup or agave syrup

1 teaspoon vanilla extract

Scant ¼ teaspoon fine sea salt

Vegan whipped cream (optional), for serving

Shaved chocolate or fresh fruit (optional), for garnish

1. In a large microwave-safe bowl, combine both milks and both chocolates. Microwave for 1 minute, whisk well, then microwave another 20 seconds. This timing should be enough to melt the chocolate. Whisk very well until it's completely smooth, all the chocolate is melted, and there are no bits remaining. If it isn't completely smooth now, your finished pots de crème will be less smooth.

2. In the bowl with the chocolate, whisk in the cashew butter, maple syrup, vanilla, and salt until completely smooth. To ensure the set dessert is as smooth as possible, transfer to a food

recipe continues »

processor and process for a few seconds to get it even smoother. The mixture will be runny, similar to chocolate milk, but don't worry, it will set in the fridge.

3. Divide the mixture evenly among four 6-ounce ramekins. Carefully place them in the fridge to chill overnight and set.

4. When ready to serve, add vegan whipped cream and chocolate shavings or fruit, if you like.

NOTES

- I strongly recommend weighing for accurate results so the pots set properly. Just follow my grams; no need to compare to cups.
- I used a combo of semisweet and bittersweet chocolate for a balance of rich, deep chocolate taste and sweetness. All bittersweet made it too bitter for me and all semisweet made it too sweet, plus it didn't set as well because it has less cocoa butter in it. I found my ratios to deliver that balance I wanted. If you prefer a darker, less sweet dessert, do half bittersweet and half semisweet. Increase the sweetener to 2 tablespoons if you choose this. Make sure you are using a bittersweet of 69% to 70% cacao.
- For the milks, I find a combo of "lite" coconut and almond yields the best result. The coconut milk adds some creamy richness with no coconut taste. I tested one with all almond milk and it wasn't quite creamy or rich enough for me.

NUTRITION (1 ramekin): 408.6 CALORIES   6.4g PROTEIN   36.8g CARBS   27.7g FAT   3.7g FIBER   24.8g SUGAR   147.3mg SODIUM

sweet potato cake

This cake is so moist and divine that it is hard to believe it is low-fat and oil-free! The magic in this cake is, of course, sweet potatoes, which lend so much moisture, but also the molasses, which makes it moist and rich in flavor. It was hard not to eat the whole thing knowing how good it was and so much healthier than a traditional cake. Sweet potatoes are loaded with vitamin A (in the form of beta-carotene). They are high in fiber, a go-to starchy carb, and excellent for skin and hair health. Being able to enjoy cake with health benefits is always a plus in my book!

¾ cup (180g) mashed cooked sweet potato (see Note), accurately measured

½ cup (120g) unsweetened almond milk

¾ cup (240g) pure maple syrup

2 tablespoons (40g) regular molasses (not blackstrap)

1¾ cups (196g) white whole wheat flour

2 tablespoons (16g) cornstarch

1½ teaspoons baking powder

1 teaspoon baking soda

1 teaspoon ground cinnamon

½ teaspoon fine sea salt

Vegan powdered sugar (optional), for serving

1. Preheat the oven to 350°F. Lightly mist an 8 × 8-inch baking dish with cooking spray.

2. In a blender or food processor, combine the mashed sweet potato, 6 tablespoons (90g) water, the almond milk, maple syrup, and molasses and blend until smooth.

3. In a large bowl, whisk together the flour, cornstarch, baking powder, baking soda, cinnamon, and salt. Pour the wet ingredients from the blender over the dry and gently fold with a spoon until just mixed, being very careful not to overmix. The batter will not be runny, but on the thicker side. Pour the batter into the prepared pan. Spread it out evenly to the corners and smooth out the top with the back of a spoon.

4. Bake until a toothpick inserted in the center of the cake comes out totally clean, about 30 minutes.

5. Let the cake cool in the pan for 1 hour at room temperature and then 30 minutes in the fridge. I know it will be hard to wait, but this cake is very moist from the sweet potato, so it's important to let

recipe continues »

it fully cool before slicing, otherwise it will be too dense and fragile if cut too early. I love this cake stored in the fridge. It is so moist that it will not dry out. Just keep it covered with foil. Dust it with powdered sugar before serving, if you'd like.

NOTE Cook sweet potatoes (with skins on) either by baking or microwaving. It will be more flavorful this way, as opposed to steaming, which adds too much moisture. To microwave, cook one potato at a time; wrap the potato with a paper towel and cook for 4 to 5 minutes until it is soft and squishy, so it will blend up beautifully (depending on the size of your sweet potato, the cooking time can vary). To bake in the oven, place the potatoes on a parchment-lined sheet pan and poke a few holes in each potato with a fork. Bake at 400°F until they are fork-tender and soft, about 45 minutes. Peel and mash the potato and be sure to weigh the exact amount required for the recipe.

NUTRITION (1 slice): 178.2 CALORIES   2.5g PROTEIN   42.8g CARBS   0.6g FAT   3.5g FIBER   20.3g SUGAR   301.6mg SODIUM

vanilla protein mug cake

I have four mug cake recipes on my website, but three of them are chocolate and the fourth is a toffee flavor. I've never created a simple vanilla one. Until now! This mug cake contains protein and fiber, and has no added oil. It is important to use a sweetened protein powder whose flavor you like, as it will affect the result. Not all protein powders taste the same, so I can only vouch for the Sprout Living vanilla powder I used. The almond flour helps to add moisture here where there is no oil. If you are allergic, try sunflower seeds ground into a flour. The tapioca starch helps to make it fluffy, acting as an egg, so do not omit. The prep time doesn't include the time to freeze the milk.

3 tablespoons (24g) superfine oat flour (gluten-free if needed)

3 tablespoons (21g) superfine blanched almond flour

1 tablespoon (9g) sweetened vanilla protein powder

1½ teaspoons tapioca starch or cornstarch

½ teaspoon baking powder

⅛ teaspoon fine sea salt

3 tablespoons (45g) unsweetened creamy plant-based milk

1 tablespoon (20g) pure maple syrup or agave syrup

¼ teaspoon vanilla extract

3 tablespoons (45g) dairy-free semisweet chocolate chips or 3 tablespoons blueberries (see Note)

NOTE Using chocolate chips will result in a higher fat content. If you would like to be a lower-fat dessert, then just use the blueberries. I do not recommend eating it without either though, as they both help to add moisture to the cake.

1. In a small bowl, whisk together the oat flour, almond flour, protein powder, tapioca starch, baking powder, and salt. Add the milk, maple syrup, and vanilla and gently whisk, being careful not to overmix. Overmixing oat-based batters can result in a dense, chewy texture. The batter will be more runny than thick. Gently stir in the chocolate chips or blueberries.

2. Pour the batter into a 10- or 12-ounce microwave-safe coffee mug. Microwave for 90 seconds until it's puffy and a toothpick comes out clean from the center.

3. Let the mug cake sit for 4 minutes before eating. This allows the cake to finish cooking and cool off some. Mug cakes are a bit moist right away, so letting them cool a few minutes results in a better texture.

NUTRITION (1 cake): 358 CALORIES   17.9g PROTEIN   45.4g CARBS   13.9g FAT   5.6g FIBER   17.8g SUGAR   591.8mg SODIUM

mint chocolate chip protein shake

This delicious, healthy mint chocolate chip protein shake is made with such wholesome plant-based ingredients, you won't believe it tastes like ice cream! This recipe is a huge reader favorite on my blog, and since it's a protein-rich recipe, I had to include it in this book. It truly does taste like mint chocolate chip ice cream. It honestly will shock you. The combo of fresh mint and extract tastes incredible! To ensure you get the right flavor result, don't skimp on following my exact gram weights given here.

1½ cups (360g) unsweetened creamy plant-based milk (I used almond)

2 handfuls of fresh spinach (30g)

Scant ¼ cup (4g) fresh mint leaves

½ large avocado

2 tablespoons (40g) pure maple syrup or preferred sweetener, plus more to taste

1 scoop (19g) sweetened vegan vanilla protein powder

⅛ to ¼ teaspoon peppermint extract

¾ cup ice cubes

2 tablespoons (30g) dairy-free bittersweet chocolate chips

1. Pour 1 cup (240g) of the milk into an ice cube tray and freeze. This will make the smoothie slushy and cold like ice cream—it really makes a difference! Weigh for accuracy if possible.

2. In a blender, combine the remaining ½ cup (120g) of milk, the frozen milk cubes, spinach, mint, avocado, maple syrup, protein powder, and ⅛ teaspoon of the mint extract, and the ice cubes. Blend until smooth and creamy. Taste and adjust the sweetener if needed (my protein powder is sweet, so I didn't need to add more syrup and it was perfect). Add more mint extract if needed, but be careful, as it can easily overpower the shake.

3. Add the chocolate chips and briefly blend so there are bits all throughout just like the ice cream.

NUTRITION: 519.3 CALORIES   20.3g PROTEIN   53.1g CARBS   25.9g FAT   8.3g FIBER   35.7g SUGAR   433.3mg SODIUM

dark chocolate orange-glazed scones

Oh, my word, these are incredible! A crispy, golden exterior with a moist, fluffy interior and pops of orange flavor that is complemented by the rich decadence of dark chocolate. These scones will wow your guests and they will never believe they are vegan or gluten-free, and without butter! These are great for a special weekend breakfast as well as being served as a dessert. They are delicious with a hot cup of coffee or tea.

SCONES

2 cups (224g) superfine blanched almond flour

½ cup (64g) superfine gluten-free oat flour

½ cup (64g) tapioca starch

1 tablespoon (8g) ground flaxseeds

2 teaspoons baking powder

¼ cup (48g) coconut sugar

½ teaspoon fine sea salt

¼ cup (80g) pure maple syrup or agave syrup

Grated zest of 1 orange

¼ cup (60g) freshly squeezed orange juice

1 teaspoon vanilla extract

½ cup (120g) dairy-free bittersweet chocolate chips (69% to 70% cacao)

ORANGE GLAZE

¼ cup (30g) vegan powdered sugar

2 teaspoons orange juice

1. Make the scones: In a large bowl, whisk together the almond flour, oat flour, tapioca starch, flaxseeds, baking powder, coconut sugar, and salt. Add the maple syrup, orange zest, orange juice, vanilla, and chocolate chips and stir until a thick dough forms. Press with the back of a spoon until it's a cohesive dough. Wrap the dough in plastic wrap and place in the freezer for 1 hour, as it will be too sticky to handle right away.

2. Preheat the oven to 375°F. Line a sheet pan with parchment paper.

3. Remove the chilled dough and form into a ball, then roll out into a round flat disc about 1 inch thick and 7 to 8 inches wide. If the dough is still a bit sticky, place another piece of parchment paper on top of the dough and roll it out. Cut the dough evenly with a very sharp knife or dough cutter into 8 equal wedges. The best way to do this is cut the disc in half first, then cut those 2 halves in half and then those 4 quarters in half again to get 8 wedges. Arrange the wedges spaced a couple of inches apart on the lined pan.

4. Bake until golden brown on the tips, 20 to 25 minutes. Let cool 20 minutes on the pan so they can firm up and set, as they will be too fragile to pick up while warm. Use a spatula to carefully transfer them to a cooling rack before glazing.

5. Meanwhile, make the orange glaze: In a small bowl, whisk the powdered sugar and orange juice together.

6. Drizzle the glaze on top of each scone and serve. Store any leftover scones in a glass container at room temperature for 2 days.

NOTE   These are best eaten the first day, as they will lose their crispiness by the next day and start to dry out after 2 days. They can be reheated in the oven to crisp them up again, if desired, at 300°F for about 5 minutes.

NUTRITION (1 scone): 326.1 CALORIES   7.7g PROTEIN   40.8g CARBS   16.5g FAT   4.3g FIBER   21.8g SUGAR   247.1mg SODIUM

sweet potato caramel

This caramel is one of the easiest and most delicious desserts you'll ever try. It's a unique and much better for you way to make caramel! It doesn't use any cream or butter like traditional caramel, but is actually made with sweet potatoes! Even though it's low-fat, it tastes incredible, and I promise you will become hooked. I love to serve this caramel over vanilla ice cream. However, it is also delicious on pancakes, waffles, cake, brownies, etc.!

¼ cup (60g) mashed cooked sweet potato (see Note, page 225)

½ cup (120g) unsweetened creamy plant-based milk (I used almond)

¼ cup (48g) coconut sugar **(do not substitute with another sugar or it won't taste like caramel!)**

¼ teaspoon ground cinnamon (optional)

¼ teaspoon fine sea salt

¼ teaspoon vanilla extract

1. In a blender, combine all the ingredients and blend until completely smooth.

2. Pour the mixture into a small pot, set over medium-low heat, and bring to a simmer. Stir with a silicone spoon or spatula until it thickens up and coats the back of the spoon, a couple of minutes or more.

3. Remove from the heat and let it cool in the pot. Note that the caramel will thicken up much more as it cools, so don't worry if it's not as thick as you want directly after cooking. It will also thicken up even more in the fridge after a few hours or overnight. Simply reheat in the microwave for 30 seconds to 1 minute before using to make it easier to pour.

NUTRITION (¼ cup): 61 CALORIES   0.4g PROTEIN   14.8g CARBS   0.3g FAT   0.5g FIBER   12.5g SUGAR   148.9mg SODIUM

frozen strawberry yogurt bark with dark chocolate

Strawberries and chocolate is one of my favorite combinations. The contrast of the tart and sweet fruit with the deep, rich flavor of dark chocolate is addictive. Frozen yogurt is nothing new, but I wanted to amp up that basic flavor profile. Using freeze-dried strawberries gives a richer strawberry flavor and a more vibrant color.

1 (28-ounce) package freeze-dried strawberries (not fresh!)

½ cup (120g) unsweetened creamy plant-based milk (I used almond)

6 tablespoons (90g) plain or vanilla nondairy yogurt, preferably high fat

¼ cup (64g) raw cashew butter (with no added oils/sugar)

2 tablespoons (40g) agave syrup

45 grams dark chocolate (half of a 3.16-ounce bar), finely chopped

1. In a food processor, process the freeze-dried strawberries to a fine powder. Add the milk, yogurt, cashew butter, and agave and blend until completely smooth. You'll need to scrape down the sides a few times to ensure the strawberries are fully blended into a smooth, creamy consistency.

2. Line a 9 × 5-inch loaf pan or similar size pan with plastic wrap or parchment paper cut to fit the pan and lie flat. Pour the yogurt mixture into the pan. Top with the chopped chocolate. Place in the freezer to firm up for a couple of hours.

3. Use a sharp knife to slice into 10 bars. (If it was frozen overnight, let it sit at room temperature for a few minutes before cutting.)

4. Store leftover pieces in freezer well wrapped to prevent ice crystals forming.

NUTRITION (1 bar): 401.2 CALORIES   1.7g PROTEIN   85.1g CARBS   6.8g FAT   2g FIBER   70.4g SUGAR   240.1mg SODIUM

strawberry orange sorbet

Get ready to have happy taste buds! The combo of strawberries and freshly squeezed orange juice is so incredible. Not only do you get the nutritional benefit of all the vitamins by using real fruit here, it also means you don't need as much sweetener as in traditional ice cream. It is the perfect dessert when you want something sweet, but light. Sorbet is a great fat-free dessert because it is made with just fruit and water, unlike ice cream, which requires high-fat milk or cream. It is fantastic during the summer, too. Using an ice cream maker will ensure a better texture, so make sure your ice cream bowl is chilled a full 24 hours before making the recipe. You can still make it without one, but it will not be quite as smooth.

4 heaping cups (630g) hulled strawberries (be sure to weigh after hulling)

6 tablespoons (90g) freshly squeezed orange juice (do not use store-bought orange juice!)

3 tablespoons (60g) pure maple syrup

1 teaspoon (5g) vanilla extract

NOTE To freeze without an ice cream maker, pour the mixture into a freezer-safe container that can be sealed tightly with a lid. Place in the freezer and remove the sorbet once every hour, stirring the mixture around until it's solid enough to scoop. This stirring method won't work to produce as smooth a result as an ice cream maker, but it will help to prevent some of the ice crystals from forming.

1. In a blender, combine ½ cup (120g) water, the strawberries, orange juice, maple syrup, and vanilla and blend until completely smooth.

2. Transfer the mixture to a bowl and chill in the fridge for a couple of hours. This ensures it is very cold before adding to the ice cream maker. (If not using an ice cream maker, see the Note for freezing instructions.)

3. Pour the chilled mixture into an ice cream maker (see Note) and churn until it reaches a slushy-like texture, 20 to 25 minutes. Transfer to a container with a tight-fitting lid and freeze for 2 to 3 hours until firm enough to scoop.

4. Freeze any leftovers and keep in mind, since there is no fat in the sorbet, it will freeze very hard. Remove from the freezer several minutes before eating so it is soft enough to scoop again.

NUTRITION (½ cup): 102.6 CALORIES   1.2g PROTEIN   24.6g CARBS   0.5g FAT   3.2g FIBER   18.8g SUGAR   3.7mg SODIUM

4-ingredient peanut butter cookies

This is my most popular cookie recipe of all time—for good reason, too! Not only do these cookies have an amazing taste and texture, they take just 20 minutes with four main ingredients to make. I knew they needed a spot in this book for the whole world to discover these cookies!

1 cup (112g) superfine blanched almond flour

½ cup (128g) creamy natural peanut butter (see Note)

¼ cup (80g) pure maple syrup

3 tablespoons (36g) coconut sugar

1. Preheat the oven to 375°F. Line a sheet pan with parchment paper.

2. In a large bowl, stir together the almond flour, peanut butter, and maple syrup until the dough comes together into a very thick ball.

3. Add the coconut sugar to a separate bowl or plate. Divide the dough into 12 equal portions using a cookie scooper and roll each into a ball. Coat each ball well in the coconut sugar. Arrange the balls on the lined pan about 2 inches apart. Press down each cookie gently with the back of a fork in a crisscross pattern. Don't completely flatten them; they should be a little less than ½ inch thick.

4. Bake until the edges are golden brown and the tops have slightly cracked, 8 to 10 minutes. Do not overbake or they can turn dry.

5. Let the cookies cool for 10 minutes on the pan, then use a thin metal spatula to transfer to a wire rack to cool completely. If you try to remove them while still warm or with your fingers, they will fall apart. They should be slightly crispy on the outside and moist on the inside and will crisp up as they cool.

NOTE The peanut butter should have no added sugars or oils. Mine contained a trace amount of salt, but if yours doesn't, add ¼ teaspoon fine sea salt to the dough.

NUTRITION (1 cookie): 139 CALORIES 3.9g PROTEIN 10.3g CARBS 9.5g FAT 1.5g FIBER 6.9g SUGAR 49mg SODIUM

go-to sauces, spices, and staples

Lemon Herb Tahini Sauce 243

Rosemary Lemon Cream 244

Nacho Cheese Sauce 247

Easy Teriyaki Sauce 248

Texas BBQ Sauce 251

Easiest Ever Pizza Sauce 252

Lime Yogurt Chive Sauce 255

Swedish Gravy 256

Curry Powder 259

Poultry Seasoning 260

BBQ Seasoning 263

Cajun Seasoning 264

Lemon Parmesan Cheese 267

The Best Vegan Mozzarella Cheese Ever 268

Greek-Inspired Feta Cheese 271

Healthy Ketchup 274

All-Purpose Smoky Tofu 277

lemon herb tahini sauce

The green color of this sauce is gorgeous, but even better, it tastes incredible. It is creamy and tangy from the lemon juice and mustard, but really fresh from the fresh basil and parsley. This sauce goes great over potatoes and roasted veggies and makes a great healthy fat to add to meals. It's delicious served with the Chickpea and Veggie Pita Pockets (page 94).

½ cup (14g) firmly packed fresh basil leaves

1 cup (17g) lightly packed fresh parsley

¼ cup (64g) runny tahini (see Note)

3 tablespoons (45g) fresh lemon juice

2 teaspoons Dijon mustard

1½ teaspoons maple syrup or agave syrup

¼ teaspoon garlic powder

¼ teaspoon fine sea salt, plus more to taste

Few dashes freshly ground black pepper

In a blender or food processor, combine all the ingredients and ¼ cup (60g) water and blend until completely smooth and it turns a beautiful green color. Scrape down the sides a couple of times to get the mixture to combine. Taste and add more salt, if desired.

NOTE Make sure you are using a good-quality smooth and runny tahini and not one of those chunky, dry ones. It should be very runny and pour easily. This will make a huge difference in the flavor and texture of the sauce. I love both the Soom brand and Prince brand.

NUTRITION (¼ cup): 108.7 CALORIES 3.1g PROTEIN 6.5g CARBS 8.8g FAT 1.8g FIBER 2g SUGAR 170mg SODIUM

rosemary lemon cream

I'm a huge fan of rosemary. The aroma and flavor it adds to recipes is unforgettable. Since rosemary is quite piney, blending it with bright lemon balances it out nicely. It is fantastic served with the Rosemary-Infused Sweet Potato Tofu Patties (page 159). If you don't like rosemary, you could try another herb like fresh dill. Please keep in mind that if you make the sunflower seed option, it will taste more bitter and you may need to increase the agave.

¾ cup (114g) raw cashews (see Note) or rounded ½ cup (56g) sunflower seeds

2 tablespoons (30g) fresh lemon juice, plus more to taste

½ teaspoon agave syrup

1 garlic clove (4g), peeled but whole

1 tablespoon chopped fresh rosemary, plus more to taste

¼ to ½ teaspoon fine sea salt, to taste

In a high-powered blender, combine all the ingredients and ½ cup (120g) water and blend until completely smooth. Taste and add more salt or rosemary, if desired. If you want it tangier, add more lemon juice.

NOTE If you do not have a high-powered blender (such as a Vitamix), you need to soak the cashews in a bowl of water to cover overnight. When ready to cook, drain and process in a food processor (which works better than a weak blender).

NUTRITION (¼ cup): 169.7 **CALORIES** 4.5g **PROTEIN** 10.9g **CARBS** 13.3g **FAT** 1g **FIBER** 2.2g **SUGAR** 125.9mg **SODIUM**

nacho cheese sauce

Finally, a nacho cheese sauce that is actually made with healthy ingredients and no dairy, but tastes absolutely incredible! I like to literally eat this with a spoon because it's so amazing. The combination of red bell peppers, jalapeños, cashews, and salsa adds smoky, cheesy, and creamy magic to this nacho sauce. This will make your nachos taste better than ever! In addition to serving over nachos, use it as a dipping sauce with chips or in tacos and burritos.

½ cup raw cashews (75g) or sunflower seeds (56g)

⅓ cup plus 2 tablespoons (105g) hot water

½ cup (120g) mild salsa

1½ teaspoons fresh lemon juice

½ cup (60g) roasted red pepper (from a jar or homemade)

3 tablespoons (45g) brine from a jar of pickled jalapeños, mild or hot

⅓ cup (55g) hot cooked rice

2 teaspoons chili powder

1 teaspoon garlic powder

½ teaspoon fine sea salt

2 to 4 tablespoons finely chopped pickled jalapeños

1. Bring a small pot of water to a boil. Add the cashews and cook for 10 minutes. This process will make them easier to blend since this is a thick cheese sauce. Drain.

2. In a high-powered blender or food processor, combine the cashews, hot water, salsa, lemon juice, roasted pepper, jalapeño brine, rice, chili powder, garlic powder, and salt and blend until completely smooth and no grittiness remains from the nuts. You will need to scrape down the sides a few times in between blending, to get it all smooth.

3. Transfer to a bowl and stir in the chopped jalapeños.

NUTRITION (½ cup): 141.6 CALORIES   4g PROTEIN   13.5g CARBS   9g FAT   2.1g FIBER   2.8g SUGAR   584.9mg SODIUM

easy teriyaki sauce

Meet my new go-to teriyaki sauce. I have another recipe in my first cookbook, but this one relies on soy sauce instead of coconut aminos, so it's a bit more convenient. I love this teriyaki sauce so much because it comes together in literally 10 minutes and is absolutely delicious in recipes. It's salty and sweet with a touch of vinegar and heat to balance it all out perfectly. Use it in my Teriyaki Stuffed Bell Peppers (page 187) and the Teriyaki Orzo Casserole (page 100).

½ cup plus 2 tablespoons (150g) reduced-sodium soy sauce

7 tablespoons (140g) agave syrup

1 tablespoon (15g) rice vinegar

1 teaspoon garlic powder

¾ teaspoon ground ginger

½ teaspoon onion powder

⅛ to ¼ teaspoon cayenne pepper, to taste

1½ tablespoons (12g) cornstarch

1. In a bowl, combine the soy sauce, ½ cup (120g) water, the agave, rice vinegar, garlic powder, ginger, onion powder, cayenne, and cornstarch and whisk really well, making sure all the cornstarch has dissolved.

2. Add the sauce to a small pot and bring to a simmer over medium-low heat. Once simmering, let cook undisturbed, for about 5 minutes. It should have slightly thickened. Don't worry, it will thicken to the perfect consistency as it cools.

3. Remove from the heat and let cool for 30 minutes. It will thicken a lot more as it cools and then can be used for recipes.

NUTRITION (¼ cup): 105.7 CALORIES   2.2g PROTEIN   24g CARBS   0.2g FAT   0.3g FIBER   17.3g SUGAR   724.1mg SODIUM

texas bbq sauce

Here in Texas, we know good barbecue sauce! This is much healthier than using versions with ketchup, as those tend to have lots of added sugar. This version has a delicious blend of sweet, smoky, tangy, and slightly spicy. Be sure to use this sauce on the BBQ Jackfruit Cheese Pizzas (page 181)! I also love to use this over pinto beans and heat through or over veggie burgers, fries, potatoes, etc.

2 cups (480g) plain tomato sauce/passata

¼ cup (80g) pure maple syrup

3 tablespoons (45g) vegan Worcestershire sauce

2 tablespoons (40g) regular molasses (not blackstrap)

2 tablespoons (30g) apple cider vinegar

2 tablespoons (30g) liquid smoke

1½ tablespoons chili powder

1 tablespoon garlic powder

½ teaspoon freshly ground black pepper

¼ teaspoon fine sea salt

½ teaspoon ground espresso (optional)

1. In a blender or food processor, combine all the ingredients and process until smooth.

2. Add the sauce to a pot and bring to simmer over medium heat. Once simmering, cook, whisking constantly for 3 to 5 minutes until the spices cook through and it is warmed throughout.

3. You can use this right away, of course, but the flavors truly enhance to an amazing flavor by chilling overnight!

NUTRITION (¼ cup): 54.8 CALORIES   0.9g PROTEIN   13.2g CARBS   0.3g FAT   1.3g FIBER   10.1g SUGAR   156.8mg SODIUM

easiest ever pizza sauce

You don't ever need to buy jarred pizza sauce again. My version takes just 5 minutes to make and has no added oil. I have used this sauce for years and use it weekly to make homemade pizza. My daughter and I love it. It is also great over pasta and garnished with fresh basil!

2 cups (480g) plain tomato sauce/passata

1½ teaspoons dried oregano

1½ teaspoons dried basil

1 teaspoon onion powder

1 teaspoon garlic powder

½ teaspoon dried thyme

¼ teaspoon freshly ground black pepper

1½ teaspoons pure maple syrup

¼ to ½ teaspoon fine sea salt (depending on if your tomato sauce is salted)

¼ teaspoon red pepper flakes

In a blender or food processor, combine all the ingredients and blend until completely smooth. This sauce will keep for 2 weeks in the fridge or in the freezer for 3 months. It will thicken up a lot in the fridge (since it is oil-free), so give it a good whisk before use. If frozen, thaw and warm up over low heat before using.

NUTRITION (¼ cup): 21 CALORIES   1g PROTEIN   4.9g CARBS   0.2g FAT   1.1g FIBER   3.5g SUGAR   129mg SODIUM

lime yogurt chive sauce

This sauce goes great with so many savory dishes and even on top of chili. Since this sauce is tangy, it is also a great complement to spicy dishes like burritos or tacos. I like it with the Veggie-Packed Lentil Rice Patties (page 156). I used the Kite Hill plain almond yogurt. It's very thick and creamy. I suggest, if possible, making this a day ahead of time, as the flavor really intensifies as it sits overnight.

½ cup (120g) plain nondairy yogurt

Grated zest of 1 lime

1 tablespoon (15g) fresh lime juice, plus more to taste

¼ teaspoon garlic powder

1 teaspoon pure maple syrup

¼ teaspoon fine sea salt, plus more to taste

Freshly ground black pepper

1 heaping tablespoon minced fresh chives

In a medium bowl, whisk together the yogurt, lime zest, lime juice, garlic powder, maple syrup, salt, a few grinds of pepper, and the chives until smooth. Taste and add more lime juice if you want it tangier and salt, if needed. This amount can vary depending on the brand of yogurt used. Chill in the fridge for a few hours before serving if you have time.

NUTRITION (2 tablespoons): 22.3 CALORIES   0.3g PROTEIN   3.6g CARBS   0.9g FAT   0.6g FIBER   1.6g SUGAR   126.8mg SODIUM

swedish gravy

This gravy is so good and full of flavor! You may just be tempted to eat it with a spoon. While I created it to be served with the Swedish Meatballs (page 178), it would also be delicious on mashed potatoes or drizzled over roasted broccoli. Be sure to use a creamy plant-based milk, because if the milk is too watery, the gravy won't thicken very well.

1¼ cups (300g) unsweetened creamy plant-based milk, such as canned "lite" coconut milk

¾ cup (180g) low-sodium vegetable broth

3 tablespoons (45g) plain nondairy yogurt

1 to 2 tablespoons (15g to 30g) reduced-sodium soy sauce or coconut aminos

1 teaspoon rice vinegar

½ teaspoon garlic powder

½ teaspoon mustard powder

2 teaspoons dried onion flakes

2 tablespoons (16g) cornstarch

¼ teaspoon fine sea salt

⅛ teaspoon freshly ground black pepper

1 tablespoon chopped fresh parsley

1. In a blender, combine all the ingredients and blend until smooth.

2. Pour the mixture into a large saucepan and bring to a simmer over medium-low heat. Once simmering, whisk constantly until it thickens to desired consistency, 5 to 8 minutes. Don't overcook it or it will become too thick and won't remain saucy.

NUTRITION (¼ cup): 50.1 CALORIES   0.7g PROTEIN   5.7g CARBS   2.7g FAT   0.4g FIBER   0.9g SUGAR   133.3mg SODIUM

curry powder

Make your own curry powder at home in just minutes with dried spices. No need to use store-bought blends. My blend is so flavorful and really adds delicious dimension and flavor to curry dishes. Use it in the Butternut Squash Curry (page 93).

3 tablespoons ground turmeric

3 tablespoons ground coriander

1 tablespoon plus ½ teaspoon ground cumin

1½ teaspoons garlic powder

¾ teaspoon ground cinnamon

¾ teaspoon cayenne pepper

¾ teaspoon ground ginger

¼ teaspoon plus ⅛ teaspoon ground nutmeg

1½ teaspoons freshly ground black pepper

Good pinch of ground cloves (optional)

In a bowl, whisk together all the spices until thoroughly blended. Store in an airtight jar in the pantry for up to 6 months.

NUTRITION (1 tablespoon): 24.5 CALORIES   0.9g PROTEIN   4.9g CARBS   0.7g FAT   2.1g FIBER   0.2g SUGAR   3.5mg SODIUM

poultry seasoning

It may seem unusual to have the word *poultry* in a vegan cookbook, because obviously there is no chicken in this book. Poultry seasoning is a classic seasoning that is traditionally used on chicken, of course. But that doesn't mean that can be the only use. The spice blend is so flavorful and can add so much depth of flavor where chicken is normally in the recipe, as proven by the Veggie Pot Pie Soup (page 128).

1 tablespoon onion powder

1 tablespoon garlic powder

2 teaspoons dried basil

1 teaspoon dried rosemary

1 teaspoon ground coriander

1 teaspoon ground sage

1 teaspoon dried thyme

1½ teaspoons paprika

¾ teaspoon dried marjoram

¼ teaspoon freshly ground black pepper

In a food processor or blender, add the spices and process into a powder. Store in an airtight jar in the pantry for up to 6 months.

NUTRITION (1 tablespoon): 17.9 CALORIES   0.8g PROTEIN   3.9g CARBS   0.3g FAT   1.3g FIBER   0.2g SUGAR   3.5mg SODIUM

bbq seasoning

If you love all things barbecue, then this seasoning is meant for you! You could truly add this blend to anything you want to take on a lot of extra flavor. It could be added to soups, chili, sauces, or sprinkled on potatoes. In fact, I use it for the BBQ-Spiced Sweet Potato Fries (page 62) and it's divine.

1 tablespoon onion powder

1 tablespoon garlic powder

4 teaspoons coconut sugar

1 to 2 teaspoons chili powder, to taste

1 teaspoon smoked paprika

1 teaspoon sweet paprika

½ teaspoon chipotle chile powder

½ teaspoon fine sea salt

¼ teaspoon freshly ground black pepper

In a small bowl, combine all the spices and mix well. Store in an airtight jar in the pantry for up to 6 months.

NUTRITION (1 tablespoon): 35.5 CALORIES   0.9g PROTEIN   8.1g CARBS   0.3g FAT   1g FIBER   4.4g SUGAR   264.6mg SODIUM

cajun seasoning

Make your very own homemade Cajun spice seasoning in just a few minutes with easy everyday pantry spices. This is a salt-free version so you can control the amount of sodium/salt that goes into your dish or meal. It is full of great depth of flavor and a kick of heat to enhance any recipe you add this blend to! It is the very blend that is used in the delicious Cajun Spinach Artichoke Pasta (page 188).

3 tablespoons paprika (not smoked or hot)

2 tablespoons garlic powder

1½ tablespoons onion powder

1½ tablespoons dried thyme

1½ tablespoons dried oregano

2 teaspoons ground black pepper

1½ to 2 teaspoons cayenne pepper, to taste

In a small bowl, stir together all the spices until well combined. Store in an airtight jar in the pantry for up to 6 months.

NUTRITION (1 tablespoon): 21 CALORIES   0.9g PROTEIN   4.4g CARBS   0.5g FAT   1.7g FIBER   0.4g SUGAR   2mg SODIUM

lemon parmesan cheese

Blanched almond flour has a similar texture to dairy parmesan, so it works brilliantly as a vegan parmesan. Do not confuse this flour with almond meal, which is drier and includes the skins. Blanched almond flour is moister because the almonds have been blanched to remove the skins, so aesthetically it looks like classic parmesan cheese. My favorite brands are the Higher Harvest by H-E-B, King Arthur Flour, Wellbee's, Honeyville, and Nature's Eats. You can use this recipe for any recipe in this book calling for vegan parmesan. It is also used in the Hungarian Sült Polenta Margherita (page 109). Or, of course, serve over pizza or pasta!

1 cup (112g) blanched almond flour (see Note)

2 teaspoons dried oregano
½ teaspoon fine sea salt

1 tablespoon (15g) fresh lemon juice

NOTE If you are allergic to almonds, make your own sunflower seed flour. In a food processor, grind ¾ cup (112g) raw sunflower seeds into as fine of a powder as you can get it. Keep in mind this will yield more of a sunflower taste and not quite as parmesan-like, but the lemon juice does help to mask it.

1. Preheat the oven to 350°F. Line a sheet pan with parchment paper.

2. In a small bowl, whisk together the almond flour, dried oregano, and salt. Add the lemon juice and use a fork (not a spoon) to press and mix for a couple of minutes until all the almond flour is coated evenly. It will seem too dry at first but be patient and mix for a couple of minutes or so until it becomes moist. If you add too much liquid, it will turn into a paste and be ruined. It will clump a bit, so use your fingertips to rub the mixture between your hands into a fine meal texture. Spread out on the lined pan.

3. Bake until the edges are just turning golden brown, 5 to 7 minutes. Watch closely, as it will quickly turn from golden to burnt!

4. After it has baked, cool for 5 to 10 minutes and it will have similar moisture and texture to real dairy parmesan cheese. If there are any larger clumps, break them with your fingertips. Store in a sealed container in the fridge for a couple of weeks.

NUTRITION (2 tablespoons): 83 CALORIES   3.1g PROTEIN   3.4g CARBS   7.1g FAT   1.9g FIBER   0.7g SUGAR   121.1mg SODIUM

the best vegan mozzarella cheese ever

This cheese is, by far, one of my most popular recipes. Simply put, readers go crazy over it. Most vegan cheese recipes rely on oils and thickeners or starches, but my version does not. It is a liquid mozzarella, so it's incredible on pizza, quesadillas, lasagna, and anything your heart desires. It is easy to drizzle onto any dish and firms up while it bakes beautifully. Please weigh your ingredients if possible, so you get exactly the right ratios for this cheese to turn out perfectly! You don't need to use the cups to compare measurements, just simply use my gram weights listed.

½ cup (120g) low-sodium vegetable broth

¼ cup (60g) plain high-fat nondairy yogurt

½ cup (75g) raw cashews (see Notes)

½ cup (120g) packed mashed cooked gold potato (see Notes)

¼ cup (50g) packed cooked white rice (see Notes)

½ to 1 tablespoon (15g) distilled white vinegar (see Notes)

1 teaspoon fresh lemon juice

¾ teaspoon fine sea salt

Add the broth first to a blender (this will make for easier blending). Then add the yogurt, cashews, potato, rice, vinegar, lemon juice, and salt. Blend on high until 100 percent smooth, thick, and creamy. You may need to scrape down the sides a couple of times to get it going. You can use it right away or place in the fridge to firm up a bit. Store in the fridge for up to 1 week or freeze for up to 1 month.

NOTES

- For the cashews: If you do not have a high-powered blender (such as a Vitamix), you need to soak the cashews in a bowl of water to cover overnight. When ready to cook, drain and process in a food processor (which works better than a weak blender).
- To cook the potato: I popped a couple of potatoes in the microwave wrapped in a wet paper towel and cooked until really soft. Let cool and then peel the skin off and weigh 120 grams (a packed ½ cup).

recipe continues »

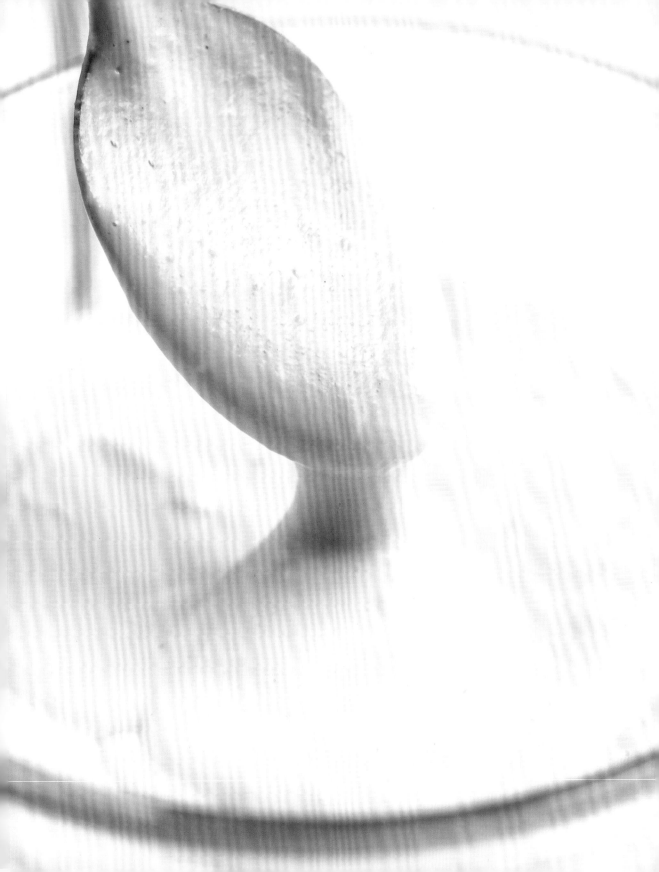

- For the rice: You can use those frozen white rice packets that cook in 3 minutes or use some already cooked white rice. Just make sure it is not cold stiff rice from the fridge, or it will be hard to blend it up smoothly. You can briefly warm it in the microwave to make sure it is a thick and sticky rice.
- Use ½ tablespoon vinegar for mild tang and 1 tablespoon for extra tang, but this ingredient is the key to the cheesy flavor, so don't substitute.

VEGAN MOZZARELLA FOR SANDWICHES: To use for a grilled cheese sandwich or in a quesadilla, the cheese should be baked first to firm it up, so it doesn't ooze all over the place. Line a 6-inch round cake pan with parchment paper, pressing it along the sides of the pan to fit flat. Pour the blended cheese sauce into the pan and bake at 350°F for 10 minutes. Remove from the oven and proceed with your recipe.

NUTRITION (¼ cup): 94 CALORIES   2.4g PROTEIN   10.3g CARBS   5.1g FAT   0.8g FIBER   0.8g SUGAR   186mg SODIUM

greek-inspired feta cheese

Nothing says delicious like tangy, cheesy, and creamy, am I right? I love creating vegan cheeses. They can be challenging, but this feta turned out really delicious. I have a few baked cheese recipes on my blog that are amazing, so I used that same baking method here for this feta. It is a fabulous addition to Tim's Greek Salad (page 66), but it could be used on any type of salad or even in soups for a cheesy note! You can eat it creamy-style (unbaked) or crumbled (baked) or firm and cubed (baked longer). Prep time does not include the tofu pressing.

1 (14-ounce) package extra-firm tofu

2 tablespoons (32g) raw cashew butter (with no added oils/sugar)

3 tablespoons (45g) fresh lemon juice

3 tablespoons (45g) rice vinegar

1 tablespoon (15g) caper brine (the juice from a jar of capers)

1 tablespoon (8g) nutritional yeast

½ teaspoon garlic powder

¾ teaspoon fine sea salt, plus more to taste

1 teaspoon dried oregano

1. Press the tofu (see Note) and let sit for 30 minutes. Squeeze as much water out as possible with paper towels so the cheese is bold and flavorful.

2. Preheat the oven to 375°F. Line a 9 × 5-inch loaf pan with parchment paper going in both directions, cut to fit so the pieces of paper lie flat with slight overhang.

3. In a food processor, combine the tofu, cashew butter, lemon juice, vinegar, caper brine, nutritional yeast, garlic powder, and salt and blend until creamy and mixed. It should be thick. Taste and add more salt, if desired. Remember, feta should be quite salty and tangy so that it stands out in recipes. Stir in the oregano. (If you stop here, you have a feta that you can spread on toast or crackers, etc.)

4. Transfer the mixture to the loaf pan. Spread out the top so it is flat. Cover loosely with foil.

recipe continues »

5. Bake until slightly golden around the edges, about 35 minutes for a softer, crumbly feta or 40 minutes for a firmer, bite-like feta.

6. Refrigerate the cheese (still in the pan) for a few hours to firm up more before slicing.

7. Once chilled, lift out the parchment paper and carefully slice the cheese into 45 bite-size pieces, about ¾ inch thick. If you prefer it crumbled (I do!), simply crumble the feta with your hands instead of slicing it.

NOTE To press tofu: Use a tofu press if you have one. Otherwise, place several layers of paper towel on a large plate or cutting board. Set the tofu on the paper towels and top with more paper towels. Place a weight (like a skillet filled with canned goods) on top to help press the water out of the tofu.

NUTRITION (¼ cup/50g): 89.9 CALORIES   7.2g PROTEIN   3.9g CARBS   5.3g FAT   1.2g FIBER   0.4g SUGAR   223.2mg SODIUM

healthy ketchup

This easy homemade ketchup is made with just seven ingredients and comes together in 10 minutes! This ketchup is free of refined sugar, low sodium, and healthier than store-bought, and it tastes amazing with vegan burgers, vegan hot dogs, with fries, or whatever you like! It would be great served with the BBQ-Spiced Sweet Potato Fries (page 62).

½ cup (120g) no-salt-added tomato paste

1 tablespoon plus 1 teaspoon (20g) distilled white vinegar (this is key to the ketchup flavor, do not substitute)

1 tablespoon (20g) pure maple syrup

½ teaspoon garlic powder

½ teaspoon onion powder

Scant ¼ teaspoon ground allspice

½ teaspoon fine sea salt

1. In a medium bowl, stir together the tomato paste, ½ cup (120g) water, the vinegar, maple syrup, garlic powder, onion powder, allspice, and salt and whisk very well for 1 to 2 minutes. You want to make sure everything is mixed thoroughly and is smooth.

2. Pour the sauce into a small pot and heat over medium heat until it starts to simmer around the edges. Set your timer for exactly 4 minutes and whisk or stir constantly with a silicone spatula. Do not walk away from the pot or it'll stick to the bottom and pop all over the place. We are cooking out the raw spice flavor and developing the classic ketchup flavor; 4 minutes is just enough time to do this. The color will slightly darken.

3. Pour the ketchup into a glass container and refrigerate for a few hours or overnight to let the flavors develop fully and get nice and chilled.

NUTRITION (2 tablespoons): 23 CALORIES   1g PROTEIN   4.4g CARBS   4g FAT   0.5g FIBER   3g SUGAR   153.4mg SODIUM

all-purpose smoky tofu

I am not joking when I say I could eat this smoky tofu every day of my life. The flavor is so bold and stands out in any dish. I could just eat it all by itself. Tofu can often be bland in its center, but not this one! The tofu soaks overnight in the marinade, resulting in very flavorful tofu. Don't skip the soaking, as this is how it will turn out so incredible. This tofu can be paired side by side with any grains, potatoes, or pastas, or in wraps with a grain or potato and some green veggies of choice and hot sauce for a complete meal packed full of plant-based nutrition.

1 (10-ounce) package firm or extra-firm tofu

3 tablespoons (45g) reduced-sodium soy sauce

1 tablespoon (15g) apple cider vinegar

1 tablespoon (15g) liquid smoke

1 tablespoon (20g) pure maple syrup or agave syrup

1 teaspoon chili powder

1 teaspoon garlic powder

1. Press the tofu (see Note) and let sit for about 15 minutes. This step is very important to keep the tofu from tasting bland.

2. Cut the tofu into ½- to ¾-inch cubes. Choose a large shallow container that will hold all the cubes of tofu with no overlap, and in which the marinade will cover the tofu.

3. In a small bowl, combine the soy sauce, vinegar, liquid smoke, maple syrup, 1 tablespoon (15g) water, the chili powder, and garlic powder and mix well. Pour the marinade over the tofu and toss gently to ensure the pieces are all coated. Make sure to spoon the marinade over **each piece** and don't rush this. You want the marinade fully on top, too, so that it soaks well into the tofu overnight. This will ensure really delicious, flavorful tofu!

4. Refrigerate overnight or for at least 8 hours. Please do not skip this step. The tofu turns out so flavorful this way.

5. Preheat the oven to 375°F. Line a sheet pan with parchment paper.

6. Arrange the tofu on the lined pan.

recipe continues »

7. Bake for 15 minutes. Flip all the cubes over. Reduce the oven temperature to 350°F and bake the tofu for another 5 to 10 minutes depending on how browned you like it. I baked it for about 6 minutes

8. Let the tofu cool for about 10 minutes and serve immediately or refrigerate for later.

NOTE   To press tofu: Use a tofu press if you have one. Otherwise, place several layers of paper towel on a large plate or cutting board. Set the tofu on the paper towels and top with more paper towels. Place a weight (like a skillet filled with canned goods) on top to help press the water out of the tofu.

NUTRITION (6 pieces): 74 CALORIES   6.6g PROTEIN   6.4g CARBS   3.1g FAT   0.6g SODIUM   1g FIBER   3.8g SUGAR

acknowledgments

There are so many incredible people in my life who helped bring this dream of a second book into reality and who I must thank. People that not only were part of the actual book creation, but also those who were there for me during the times that I was super stressed and on a strict schedule of meeting deadlines.

The one and only person who I love more than anybody in this world, my sweet daughter, Olivia. Just like with my first cookbook, you were so understanding and patient with me and my workload. Although much older now with this second book, you are even more understanding of my dedication to achieve completing this book. You respected me every single time I said I had to work or take photos, knowing it was temporary. I feel so blessed and grateful to God to have you as my daughter. You are my biggest dream come true and the person who makes me the most proud on earth. My love for you knows no bounds, sweet Pumpkin.

I would like to thank my amazing food stylist, Stephanie Bohn. We made the best team on the photo shoots that we worked on together. Your incredible expertise and amazing personality, which perfectly complemented mine, made for so much fun and magic that came through in my photography. Thank you for the gorgeous prop collection you brought to our shoots.

(P.S. You can find all about how to rent her props and work with her at The Proppe Shoppe on Instagram.)

To my editor, Katherine Leak, and my art director, Jenny Davis, and the team at Rodale Books and Penguin Random House. Thank you so much for all of your guidance, patience, and feedback throughout the creation of this book, as well as the many photography shoots. Your suggestions and help were integral in making this book a success! I feel so honored and grateful to have had you both as part of this incredible process. Thank you so much for everything.

To my lifestyle photographer, Kim Schaffer. Thank you so much for your kind spirit and the fun you brought to the set in my home. My daughter and I loved working with you and it was such a great experience. You listened to my desires and guided us both perfectly and effortlessly!

To my dance family. I love you so much. My wonderful dance teachers at Fred Astaire: Richárd (Richie) Kaszás, Tilemachos (Tim) Fatsis, Barnabas Vadon, Foteini (Faith) Pangea, Elisavet (Eli) Mantani, Hector Lara, Joshua Bradford, and Edina Kobor; and Cypress studio manager, Elena Gutierrez. To my amazing coach and bestie, Alex Armaos, I am so grateful for all your knowledge and guidance to mold me into a better dancer! Thank you for giving me so much joy through dance, and a huge stress reliever as

I navigated through the process of writing this book. Richie, Faith, Tim, Eli, Barnabas, and Elena, you constantly encouraged me and believed in me and cheered me on as I was incredibly stressed and overwhelmed. I had to reduce my dance lessons to finish my book in the last few months. This meant less time at the dance studio, but you still continuously checked on me, messaged me, sent me support and love, and believed in me! I can't express how much you all mean to me.

My amazing dance friends and community, especially Michelle Kerbow, you always cheered me on, supported me, made me laugh, checked on me, and encouraged me all the way to the finish line! I'm so grateful for your friendship and our fun nights and support while I wrote my book. I truly love you so much.

To my closest friends, Kacy Allensworth, Rachel Menzel, and Carrie Panacek, my goodness, where do I start? You are the most special friends in the whole world a girl could ask for. Kacy, I've known you my entire life practically and your friendship and constant encouragement throughout the book-writing process meant the world to me. I appreciate your advice, and you always taking my calls and being the most wonderful, loving, and supportive friend ever. I feel so eternally grateful to have such a unique friendship with you for my whole life and I love you to the moon! You have always believed in me since I was a young girl and I know I can always count on you. I love you so much.

Rachel, you are so beautiful inside and out and I'm so grateful we met through dance. You know how much you mean to me and how much you've changed my life. Every single week you cheered me on, encouraged me, believed in me, and never let me doubt myself. I couldn't see you as much toward the last few months, with fewer of our monthly date nights and outings so I could finish my book. But you never complained; you understood and always sent me encouraging words, messages to make me laugh and keep my focus. Your friendship is one that can't be put into words. I love you endlessly!

Carrie, where would I be without you being such an incredible friend and always taking my calls! I love how you are my sister from another mister. You have the best advice, even if it's tough love; you shoot it straight because you love me and that makes you an incredible friend. You are a true special gem in this world and always make me laugh. I'm so happy to have you as a special friend and you always encouraged me and rooted for me to finish the book! Love you to pieces!

To my taste testers, Estee Hammer, Nina Windhauser, Megan Jolic, Lisa Marshall, Micah Horton, Lori Barr, Jessica Eaton, Marie Roberts, Joy Jerauld, Danielle Johnson, Lori Serle, Kelly Maddy, and Danielle Doerr, thank you immensely for your time and dedication to test out these recipes in your kitchens! I'm so grateful for your feedback and the enthusiasm you had for testing out the recipes and, even more so, that you all enjoyed them! Thank you for being a part of bringing this cookbook to fruition!

index

Page numbers of photographs appear in italics.

a

agave syrup
  Apple Pie Spice Balls, *196,* 197
  Chocolate Tahini Cookies, 217–19, *218–19*
  Dark Chocolate Orange-Glazed Scones, 230–31, *231*
  Easy Teriyaki Sauce, 248, *249*
  "Honey" Lime Miso Cauliflower, *64,* 65
  Mocha Chocolate Chip Granola, 198, *199*
  Pistachio Chocolate Cups, 194, *195*
  Supremely Rich Brownie Protein Bites, *192,* 193
  Sweet and Sour Tofu with Ramen, 168–70, *169*
  Sweet Jalapeño Cornbread Waffles, *36,* 37
almond butter
  Almond Sesame Tofu and Rice, 87–89, *88*
  Apple Pie Spice Balls, *196,* 197
  Harissa Almond Pasta with Spinach, *176,* 177
  Mocha Chocolate Chip Granola, 198, *199*
almond flour
  Dark Chocolate Orange-Glazed Scones, 230–31, *231*
  4-Ingredient Peanut Butter Cookies, 238, *239*
  Lemon Parmesan Cheese, *266,* 267
  recommended brands, 267
almond milk
  Chocolate Pots de Crème, 220–22, *221*
  Mint Chocolate Chip Protein Shake, *228,* 229
  Sweet Potato Caramel, *232,* 233
almonds, slivered
  Almond Cream Strawberry Shortcakes, *214,* 215–16
apple
  Apple Pie Overnight Oats, 42, *43*
  Apple Pie Spice Balls, *196,* 197

artichoke
  Caesar Dressing, 86, *86*
  Cajun Spinach Artichoke Pasta, 188, *189*
asparagus
  Thai Green Sweet Potato Curry, 165–67, *166*
avocados
  as a healthy fat, 12, 22
  Mint Chocolate Chip Protein Shake, *228,* 229
  Skillet Chickpea Quinoa Casserole, 111–13, *112–13*
  Smoky Bean Dip, *204,* 205

b

Bab Leves, *142,* 143
Baked Pumpkin Sage Risotto, *116,* 117
Baked Zucchini Crisps, 210, *211*
bars
  Chocolate Chip Walnut Protein Bars, 46–47, *47*
basil
  Garlicky Sun-Dried Tomato and Basil Rice, *60,* 61
  Lemon Herb Tahini Sauce, *242,* 243
  Lemony White Bean Basil Toasts, *96,* 97
  Olivia's Pasta Alfredo with Fresh Basil, 81–83, *82*
  Pistachio Pesto Pasta, *76,* 77
  Poultry Seasoning, 260, *261*
barbecue
  BBQ Jackfruit Cheese Pizzas, *180,* 181–82
  BBQ Seasoning, *262,* 263
  BBQ-Spiced Sweet Potato Fries, 62, *63*
  Texas BBQ Sauce, *250,* 251
beans, black
  Cheesy Quinoa Poblano Peppers, 183–84, *185*
  Feel-Good Roasted Red Pepper Veggie Soup, 140, *141*
  Smoky Bean Dip, *204,* 205
beans, pinto
  Jackfruit Pinto Bean Chili, 134–36, *135*

  Smoky Bean Dip, *204,* 205
beans, white
  Creamy Mexican Potato and White Bean Soup, 122–24, *123*
  Hungarian Bean Soup, *142,* 143
  Lemony White Bean Basil Toasts, *96,* 97
  Minestrone Soup with a Twist, 125–27, *126–27*
  White Bean Pinwheels, 68–70, *69*
blueberries
  My Go-To Protein Berry Smoothie, 34, *35*
  Vanilla Protein Mug Cake, 226, *227*
broccoli
  Sweet and Sour Tofu with Ramen, 168–70, *169*
  Teriyaki Orzo Casserole, 100–101, *101*
  Teriyaki Stuffed Bell Peppers, *186,* 187
Brownie Protein Bites, Supremely Rich, *192,* 193
buckwheat flour
  Chocolate Protein Pancakes, 29–30, *31*
  making, 30
  type to use, 29
Butternut Squash Curry, *92,* 93

c

cabbage
  White Bean Pinwheels, 68–70, *69*
Caesar Dressing, 86, *86*
Caesar Smashed Chickpea Sandwiches, 84–86, *85*
Cajun Seasoning, 264, *265*
Cajun Spinach Artichoke Pasta, 188, *189*
cake
  Sweet Potato Cake, 223–25, *224*
  Vanilla Protein Mug Cake, 226, *227*
Caramel, Sweet Potato, *232,* 233
carrots
  Guestworthy Jackfruit Lentil Curry, 171–73, *172*

Hungarian Bean Soup, *142, 143*
Lentil Soup with Turmeric and
    Lemon, 131–33, *132*
Teriyaki Orzo Casserole, 100–101,
    101
Vegan "Tuna" Casserole, *102,* 103–4
Veggie Pot Pie Soup, 128–30, *129*
cashew butter
Apple Pie Spice Balls, *196, 197*
Chocolate Pots de Crème, 220–22,
    221
Greek-Inspired Feta Cheese,
    271–73, *272*
Pistachio Chocolate Cups, 194, *195*
Supremely Rich Brownie Protein
    Bites, *192, 193*
cashews
The Best Vegan Mozzarella Cheese
    Ever, 268–70, *269–70*
boiling before processing, 146
Caesar Dressing, 86, *86*
Creamy Mexican Potato and White
    Bean Soup, 122–24, *123*
Nacho Cheese Sauce, *246,* 247
Olivia's Pasta Alfredo with Fresh
    Basil, 81–83, *82*
Peach Cream Cheese, 38, *39*
Rosemary Lemon Cream, 244, *245*
soaking before blending, 14
Vegan "Tuna" Casserole, *102,* 103–4
cauliflower
Feel-Good Roasted Red Pepper
    Veggie Soup, 140, *141*
"Honey" Lime Miso Cauliflower, *64,* 65
cayenne pepper
Cajun Seasoning, 264, *265*
cheese
The Best Vegan Mozzarella Cheese
    Ever, 268–70, *269–70*
Greek-Inspired Feta Cheese,
    271–73, *272*
Lemon Parmesan Cheese, 167, *266*
Cheesy Lentil Pasta Bake, 114–15, *115*
Cheesy Quinoa Poblano Peppers,
    183–84, *185*
cherries, dried
Seedy Coconut Trail Mix, *200,* 201
chickpeas, 21
Butternut Squash Curry, *92,* 93
Caesar Smashed Chickpea
    Sandwiches, 84–86, *85*
Chickpea and Veggie Pita Pockets,
    94, *95*
Creamy Gochujang Chickpeas
    and Lentils with Poblano Pepper,
    78–80, *79*
Miso Sweet Potato Kale Soup, 150,
    151

My Favorite Oil-Free Hummus, 206,
    207
Pizza Chickpea Balls, *208,* 209
Skillet Chickpea Quinoa Casserole,
    111–13, *112–13*
Taco Lentil and Chickpea Lettuce
    Wraps, 90, *91*
Chili, Jackfruit Pinto Bean, 134–36,
    135
chili powder
BBQ Seasoning, *262,* 263
Chive Sauce, Lime Yogurt, *254,* 255
chocolate
Chocolate Chip Sheet Pan
    Pancakes, 26, *27–28*
Chocolate Chip Walnut Protein
    Bars, 46–47, *47*
Chocolate Lentil Protein Muffins,
    44, 45
Chocolate Pots de Crème, 220–22,
    221
Chocolate Protein Pancakes,
    29–30, *31*
Chocolate Tahini Cookies, 217–19,
    218–19
Dark Chocolate Orange-Glazed
    Scones, 230–31, *231*
Frozen Strawberry Yogurt Bark with
    Dark Chocolate, 234, *235*
Mint Chocolate Chip Protein Shake,
    228, 229
Mocha Chocolate Chip Granola,
    198, *199*
Pistachio Chocolate Cups, 194,
    195
Supremely Rich Brownie Protein
    Bites, *192,* 193
Vanilla Protein Mug Cake, 226, *227*
coconut aminos
Almond Sesame Tofu and Rice,
    87–89, *88*
Butternut Squash Curry, *92,* 93
Chickpea and Veggie Pita Pockets,
    94, *95*
Pizza Chickpea Balls, *208,* 209
Rosemary-Infused Sweet Potato
    Tofu Patties, 159–61, *160–61*
Swedish Gravy, 256, *257*
coconut flakes
Seedy Coconut Trail Mix, *200,* 201
coconut milk
Chocolate Pots de Crème, 220–22,
    221
recommended brands, 72, 165
Swedish Gravy, 256, *257*
Thai Coconut Soup, 147–49, *148*
Thai Green Sweet Potato Curry,
    165–67, *166*

coconut sugar
BBQ Seasoning, *262,* 263
4-Ingredient Peanut Butter
    Cookies, 238, *239*
Sweet Potato Caramel, *232,* 233
coffee
Mocha Chocolate Chip Granola,
    198, *199*
cookies
Chocolate Tahini Cookies, 217–19,
    218–19
4-Ingredient Peanut Butter
    Cookies, 238, *239*
coriander
Curry Powder, 258, *259*
Poultry Seasoning, 260, *261*
corn
Feel-Good Roasted Red Pepper
    Veggie Soup, 140, *141*
Jackfruit Pinto Bean Chili, 134–36,
    135
The Perfect Corn Salsa, 58, *59*
Cornbread Waffles, Sweet Jalapeño,
    36, 37
Cream Cheese, Peach, 38, *39*
Creamy Italian Dill Potato Salad,
    52, 53
Creamy Mexican Potato and White
    Bean Soup, 122–24, *123*
cucumbers
Tim's Greek Salad with Homemade
    Feta, 66–67, *67*
cumin
Curry Powder, 258, 259
curry
Butternut Squash Curry, *92,* 93
Curry Tofu Scramble, *32,* 33
Guestworthy Jackfruit Lentil Curry,
    171–73, *172*
Pureed Red Lentil Curry Kale Soup,
    137–38, *139*
Sweet Potato Curry Pasta, 174, *175*
Thai Green Sweet Potato Curry,
    165–67, *166*
Curry Powder, 258, *259*

d
Dijon mustard
Caesar Dressing, 86, *86*
dill
Creamy Italian Dill Potato Salad,
    52, 53
dips
Healthy Ketchup, 274, *275*
Smoky Bean Dip, *204,* 205
Sweet Potato and Lentil Harissa
    Dip, 50, *51*

e

edamame
Teriyaki Orzo Casserole, 100–101,
101
eggplant
Parmesan Ratatouille, 118, *119*

f

feta
Greek-Inspired Feta Cheese,
271–73, *272*
Tim's Greek Salad with Homemade
Feta, 66–67, *67*
Flatbread, Easy Go-To, 71–72, *73*
flaxseeds
Seedy Coconut Trail Mix, *200*, 201
Frozen Strawberry Yogurt Bark with
Dark Chocolate, 234, *235*

g

garlic
Garlicky Sun-Dried Tomato and Basil
Rice, *60*, 61
Garlic Lemon French Green Beans
and Tomatoes, 54, *55*
garlic powder
BBQ Seasoning, *262*, 263
Cajun Seasoning, 264, *265*
Curry Powder, *258*, 259
Poultry Seasoning, 260, *261*
gochujang
Creamy Gochujang Chickpeas
and Lentils with Poblano Pepper,
78–80, *79*
graham crackers
Apple Pie Spice Balls, *196*, 197
granola
Mocha Chocolate Chip Granola,
198, *199*
green beans, French
Garlic Lemon French Green Beans
and Tomatoes, 54, *55*
green chiles
Creamy Mexican Potato and White
Bean Soup, 122–24, *123*

h

harissa
choosing a brand, 50
Harissa Almond Pasta with Spinach,
176, 177
Sweet Potato and Lentil Harissa
Dip, 50, *51*
hearts of palm
Vegan "Tuna" Casserole, *102*, 103–4
hemp hearts
Seedy Coconut Trail Mix, *200*, 201

Hummus, My Favorite Oil-Free, 206,
207
Hungarian Bean Soup (Bab Leves),
142, 143
Hungarian Sült Polenta Margherita,
108, 109–10

j

jackfruit
BBQ Jackfruit Cheese Pizzas, *180*,
181–82
Guestworthy Jackfruit Lentil Curry,
171–73, *172*
Jackfruit Pinto Bean Chili, 134–36,
135
jalapeños
The Perfect Corn Salsa, 58, *59*
Smoky Bean Dip, *204*, 205
Sweet Jalapeño Cornbread Waffles,
36, 37

k

kale
Feel-Good Roasted Red Pepper
Veggie Soup, 140, *141*
Miso Sweet Potato Kale Soup, 150,
151
Pureed Red Lentil Curry Kale Soup,
137–38, *139*
Ketchup, Healthy, 274, *275*

l

lemon/lemon juice
Caesar Dressing, 86, *86*
Garlic Lemon French Green Beans
and Tomatoes, 54, *55*
Lemon Herb Tahini Sauce, *242*, 243
Lemon Parmesan Cheese, *266*, 267
Lemony White Bean Basil Toasts,
96, 97
Lentil Soup with Turmeric and
Lemon, 131–33, *132*
Rosemary Lemon Cream, 244,
245
lentils
Cheesy Lentil Pasta Bake, 114–15,
115
Chocolate Lentil Protein Muffins,
44, 45
Creamy Gochujang Chickpeas
and Lentils with Poblano Pepper,
78–80, *79*
Guestworthy Jackfruit Lentil Curry,
171–73, *172*
Lentil Soup with Turmeric and
Lemon, 131–33, *132*

Pureed Red Lentil Curry Kale Soup,
137–38, *139*
Smoky Red Lentil Soup, *152*, 153
Swedish Meatballs, 178, *179*
Sweet Potato and Lentil Harissa
Dip, 50, *51*
Taco Lentil and Chickpea Lettuce
Wraps, 90, *91*
Veggie-Packed Lentil Rice Patties,
156–58, *157*
Lettuce Wraps, Taco Lentil and
Chickpea, 90, *91*
lime/lime juice
"Honey" Lime Miso Cauliflower,
64, 65
Lime Yogurt Chive Sauce, *254*, 255
Sweet and Sour Tofu with Ramen,
168–70, *169*

m

Mac 'n' Cheese, Protein-Packed,
162–64, *163*
maple syrup
Chocolate Chip Sheet Pancakes,
26, 27–28
Chocolate Tahini Cookies, 217–19,
218–19
Dark Chocolate Orange-Glazed
Scones, 230–31, *231*
4-Ingredient Peanut Butter
Cookies, 238, *239*
Pecan Pie Baked Oatmeal, *40*, 41
Pistachio Chocolate Cups, 194, *195*
Seedy Coconut Trail Mix, *200*, 201
Sweet Jalapeño Cornbread Waffles,
36, 37
marjoram
Poultry Seasoning, 260, *261*
Minestrone Soup with a Twist, 125–27,
126–27
Mint Chocolate Chip Protein Shake,
228, 229
miso
"Honey" Lime Miso Cauliflower,
64, 65
Miso Mashed Sweet Potatoes,
56, 57
Miso Sweet Potato Kale Soup, 150,
151
Mocha Chocolate Chip Granola, 198,
199
mozzarella cheese
BBQ Jackfruit Cheese Pizzas, *180*,
181–82
The Best Vegan Mozzarella Cheese
Ever, 268–70, *269–70*

Cheesy Lentil Pasta Bake, 114–15, *115*

Cheesy Quinoa Poblano Peppers, 183–84, *185*

Hungarian Sült Polenta Margherita, *108*, 109–10

muffins

Chocolate Chip Walnut Protein Bars (alternative), 46–47, *47*

Chocolate Lentil Protein Muffins, *44*, 45

mushrooms

Tom Kha Soup with Tofu (Thai Coconut Soup), 147–49, *148*

My Go-To Protein Berry Smoothie, 34, *35*

n

Nacho Cheese Sauce, *246*, 247

o

oats

Apple Pie Overnight Oats, 42, *43*

Apple Pie Spice Balls, *196*, 197

Mocha Chocolate Chip Granola, 198, *199*

Pecan Pie Baked Oatmeal, *40*, 41

Pistachio Chocolate Cups, 194, *195*

Swedish Meatballs, 178, *179*

olives

Tim's Greek Salad with Homemade Feta, 66–67, *67*

Olivia's Pasta Alfredo with Fresh Basil, 81–83, *82*

onion powder

BBQ Seasoning, *262*, 263

Cajun Seasoning, 264, *265*

Poultry Seasoning, 260, *261*

onions

how to sauté with water, 13–14

Minestrone Soup with a Twist, 125–27, *126–27*

Parmesan Ratatouille, 118, *119*

The Perfect Corn Salsa, 58, *59*

Tim's Greek Salad with Homemade Feta, 66–67, *67*

orange/orange juice

Dark Chocolate Orange-Glazed Scones, 230–31, *231*

Orange Glaze, 230

Strawberry Orange Sorbet, *236*, 237

oregano

Cajun Seasoning, 264, *265*

Lemon Parmesan Cheese, *266*, 267

p

pancakes

Chocolate Chip Sheet Pan Pancakes, *26*, 27–28

Chocolate Protein Pancakes, 29–30, *31*

paprika

BBQ Seasoning, *262*, 263

Cajun Seasoning, 264, *265*

Poultry Seasoning, 260, *261*

parmesan cheese

Hungarian Sült Polenta Margherita, *108*, 109–10

Lemon Parmesan Cheese, *266*, 267

Parmesan Ratatouille, 118, *119*

parsley

Lemon Herb Tahini Sauce, *242*, 243

pasta

Cajun Spinach Artichoke Pasta, 188, *189*

Cheesy Lentil Pasta Bake, 114–15, *115*

Comforting Sun-Dried Tomato and Zucchini Lasagna Soup, 144–46, *145*

Harissa Almond Pasta with Spinach, *176*, 177

Minestrone Soup with a Twist, 125–27, *126–27*

Olivia's Pasta Alfredo with Fresh Basil, 81–83, *82*

Pistachio Pesto Pasta, *76*, 77

Protein-Packed Mac 'n' Cheese, 162–64, *163*

Sweet Potato Curry Pasta, 174, *175*

Teriyaki Orzo Casserole, 100–101, *101*

Vegan "Tuna" Casserole, *102*, 103–4

Peach Cream Cheese, 38, *39*

Peanut Butter Cookies, 4-Ingredient, *238*, 239

peas

Teriyaki Orzo Casserole, 100–101, *101*

Vegan "Tuna" Casserole, *102*, 103–4

Veggie Pot Pie Soup, 128–30, *129*

pecans

Pecan Pie Baked Oatmeal, *40*, 41

Pecan Stuffing, 105–6, *107*

pepper, black

Cajun Seasoning, 264, *265*

Poultry Seasoning, 260, *261*

peppers, bell

Chickpea and Veggie Pita Pockets, *94*, 95

Feel-Good Roasted Red Pepper Veggie Soup, 140, *141*

The Perfect Corn Salsa, 58, *59*

Sweet and Sour Tofu with Ramen, 168–70, *169*

Teriyaki Stuffed Bell Peppers, *186*, 187

Tim's Greek Salad with Homemade Feta, 66–67, *67*

Pinwheels, White Bean, 68–70, *69*

pistachios

Mocha Chocolate Chip Granola, 198, *199*

Pistachio Chocolate Cups, 194, *195*

Pistachio Pesto Pasta, *76*, 77

Pita Pockets, Chickpea and Veggie, *94*, 95

pizza

BBQ Jackfruit Cheese Pizzas, *180*, 181–82

Pizza Chickpea Balls, *208*, 209

pizza sauce

Cheesy Lentil Pasta Bake, 114–15, *115*

Easiest Ever Pizza Sauce, 252, *253*

poblano peppers

Cheesy Quinoa Poblano Peppers, 183–84, *185*

Creamy Gochujang Chickpeas and Lentils with Poblano Pepper, 78–80, *79*

polenta

Hungarian Sült Polenta Margherita, *108*, 109–10

potatoes

The Best Vegan Mozzarella Cheese Ever, 268–70, *269–70*

Creamy Italian Dill Potato Salad, 52, 53

Creamy Mexican Potato and White Bean Soup, 122–24, *123*

Feel-Good Roasted Red Pepper Veggie Soup, 140, *141*

Olivia's Pasta Alfredo with Fresh Basil, 81–83, *82*

Protein-Packed Mac 'n' Cheese, 162–64, *163*

Veggie Pot Pie Soup, 128–30, *129*

Poultry Seasoning, 260, *261*

protein powder, 21

Chocolate Chip Walnut Protein Bars, 46–47, *47*

Chocolate Protein Pancakes, 29–30, *31*

choosing a brand, 21

in desserts, 21

Mint Chocolate Chip Protein Shake, *228*, 229

My Go-To Protein Berry Smoothie, 34, *35*

protein powder *(continued)*
  Supremely Rich Brownie Protein
    Bites, *192,* 193
  Vanilla Protein Mug Cake, *226, 227*
  Protein-Rich BBQ Sesame Tofu Bites,
    202, *203*
pumpkin
  Baked Pumpkin Sage Risotto, *116,* 117
pumpkin seeds
  Seedy Coconut Trail Mix, *200,*
    201

q

quinoa
  Cheesy Quinoa Poblano Peppers,
    183–84, *185*
  Skillet Chickpea Quinoa Casserole,
    111–13, *112–13*
  Teriyaki Stuffed Bell Peppers, *186,*
    187

r

ramen noodles
  Sweet and Sour Tofu with Ramen,
    168–70, *169*
rice
  Almond Sesame Tofu and Rice,
    87–89, *88*
  Baked Pumpkin Sage Risotto, *116,* 117
  Garlicky Sun-Dried Tomato and Basil
    Rice, *60,* 61
  Swedish Meatballs, 178, *179*
  Teriyaki Stuffed Bell Peppers, *186,*
    187
  Veggie-Packed Lentil Rice Patties,
    156–58, *157*
rosemary
  Poultry Seasoning, 260, *261*
  Rosemary-Infused Sweet Potato
    Tofu Patties, 159–61, *160–61*
  Rosemary Lemon Cream, 244, *245*

s

sage
  Baked Pumpkin Sage Risotto, *116,* 117
  Pecan Stuffing, 105–6, *107*
  Poultry Seasoning, 260, *261*
Salad with Homemade Feta, Tim's
    Greek, 66–67, *67*
Salsa, The Perfect Corn, 58, *59*
Sandwiches, Caesar Smashed
    Chickpea, 84–86, *85*
sauces
  Easiest Ever Pizza Sauce, 252, *253*
  Easy Teriyaki Sauce, 248, *249*
  Healthy Ketchup, 274, *275*
  Lemon Herb Tahini Sauce, *242,* 243

Lime Yogurt Chive Sauce, *254,* 255
  Nacho Cheese Sauce, *246,* 247
  Rosemary Lemon Cream, 244, *245*
  Swedish Gravy, 256, *257*
  Texas BBQ Sauce, *250,* 251
Scones, Dark Chocolate
    Orange-Glazed, 230–31, *231*
seasonings
  BBQ Seasoning, *262,* 263
  Cajun Seasoning, *264,* 265
  Curry Powder, *258,* 259
  Poultry Seasoning, 260, *261*
Seedy Coconut Trail Mix, *200,* 201
sesame
  Almond Sesame Tofu and Rice,
    87–89, *88*
  Protein-Rich BBQ Sesame Tofu
    Bites, 202, *203*
Shake, Mint Chocolate Chip Protein,
    228, 229
Shortcakes, Almond Cream
    Strawberry, *214,* 215–16
Skillet Chickpea Quinoa Casserole,
    111–13, *112–13*
Smoky Bean Dip, *204,* 205
Smoky Red Lentil Soup, *152,* 153
Smoky Tofu, All-Purpose, *276, 277–78*
Smoothie, My Go-To Protein Berry,
    34, *35*
Sorbet, Strawberry Orange, *236,* 237
soups
  Comforting Sun-Dried Tomato and
    Zucchini Lasagna Soup, 144–46,
    145
  Creamy Mexican Potato and White
    Bean Soup, 122–24, *123*
  Feel-Good Roasted Red Pepper
    Veggie Soup, 140, *141*
  Hungarian Bean Soup, *142,* 143
  Lentil Soup with Turmeric and
    Lemon, 131–33, *132*
  Minestrone Soup with a Twist, 125–
    27, *126–27*
  Miso Sweet Potato Kale Soup, 150,
    151
  Pureed Red Lentil Curry Kale Soup,
    137–38, *139*
  Smoky Red Lentil Soup, *152,* 153
  Tom Kha Soup with Tofu (Thai
    Coconut Soup), 147–49, *148*
  Veggie Pot Pie Soup, 128–30, *129*
soy sauce (low-sodium)
  Easy Teriyaki Sauce, 248, *249*
  Swedish Gravy, 256, *257*
spinach
  Cajun Spinach Artichoke Pasta,
    188, *189*

Chickpea and Veggie Pita Pockets,
    94, *95*
  Harissa Almond Pasta with Spinach,
    176, 177
  Lentil Soup with Turmeric and
    Lemon, 131–33, *132*
  Pistachio Pesto Pasta, *76,* 77
  Skillet Chickpea Quinoa Casserole,
    111–13, *112–13*
  Smoky Red Lentil Soup, *152,* 153
strawberries
  Almond Cream Strawberry
    Shortcakes, *214,* 215–16
  Frozen Strawberry Yogurt Bark with
    Dark Chocolate, 234, *235*
  My Go-To Protein Berry Smoothie,
    34, *35*
  Strawberry Orange Sorbet, *236,*
    237
Stuffing, Pecan, 105–6, *107*
Swedish Gravy, 256, *257*
Swedish Meatballs, 178, *179*
Sweet and Sour Tofu with Ramen,
    168–70, *169*
sweet potatoes
  BBQ-Spiced Sweet Potato Fries,
    62, *63*
  Miso Mashed Sweet Potatoes,
    56, 57
  Miso Sweet Potato Kale Soup, 150,
    151
  Rosemary-Infused Sweet Potato
    Tofu Patties, 159–61, *160–61*
  Sweet Potato and Lentil Harissa
    Dip, 50, *51*
  Sweet Potato Cake, 223–25, *224*
  Sweet Potato Caramel, *232,* 233
  Sweet Potato Curry Pasta, 174, *175*
  Thai Green Sweet Potato Curry,
    165–67, *166*

t

Taco Lentil and Chickpea Lettuce
    Wraps, 90, *91*
tahini
  Chocolate Tahini Cookies, 217–19,
    218–19
  Lemon Herb Tahini Sauce, *242, 243*
  My Favorite Oil-Free Hummus, 206,
    207
  recommended brands, 206
Teriyaki Orzo Casserole, 100–101, *101*
Teriyaki Sauce, Easy, 248, *249*
Teriyaki Stuffed Bell Peppers, *186,* 187
Texas BBQ Sauce, *250,* 251
Thai Coconut Soup, 147–49, *148*

Thai Green Sweet Potato Curry, 165–67, *166*
thyme
  Cajun Seasoning, 264, *265*
  Pecan Stuffing, 105–6, *107*
  Poultry Seasoning, 260, *261*
Tim's Greek Salad with Homemade Feta, 66–67, *67*
Toasts, Lemony White Bean Basil, *96*, 97
tofu
  All-Purpose Smoky Tofu, *276*, 277–78
  Almond Sesame Tofu and Rice, 87–89, *88*
  Curry Tofu Scramble, *32*, 33
  Greek-Inspired Feta Cheese, 271–73, *272*
  pressing, 20
  Protein-Packed Mac 'n' Cheese, 162–64, *163*
  Protein-Rich BBQ Sesame Tofu Bites, 202, *203*
  Rosemary-Infused Sweet Potato Tofu Patties, 159–61, *160–61*
  Sweet and Sour Tofu with Ramen, 168–70, *169*
  Teriyaki Orzo Casserole, 100–101, *101*
  Tom Kha Soup with Tofu (Thai Coconut Soup), 147–49, *148*
tomatoes
  Garlic Lemon French Green Beans and Tomatoes, 54, *55*
  Parmesan Ratatouille, 118, *119*

Tim's Greek Salad with Homemade Feta, 66–67, *67*
tomatoes, canned fire-roasted
  Hungarian Sült Polenta Margherita, *108*, 109–10
  Parmesan Ratatouille, 118, *119*
  Skillet Chickpea Quinoa Casserole, 111–13, *112–13*
tomatoes, sun-dried
  Comforting Sun-Dried Tomato and Zucchini Lasagna Soup, 144–46, *145*
  Garlicky Sun-Dried Tomato and Basil Rice, *60*, 61
  Pizza Chickpea Balls, *208*, 209
tomato sauce/passata
  Comforting Sun-Dried Tomato and Zucchini Lasagna Soup, 144–46, *145*
  Easiest Ever Pizza Sauce, 252, *253*
  Minestrone Soup with a Twist, 125–27, *126–27*
  Pizza Chickpea Balls, *208*, 209
  Texas BBQ Sauce, *250*, 251
  Tom Kha Soup with Tofu (Thai Coconut Soup), 147–49, *148*
tortillas
  Veggie Pot Pie Soup, 128–30, *129*
  White Bean Pinwheels, 68–70, *69*
Trail Mix, Seedy Coconut, *200*, 201
"Tuna" Casserole, Vegan, *102*, 103–4
turmeric
  Curry Powder, *258*, 259
  Lentil Soup with Turmeric and Lemon, 131–33, *132*

V
Vanilla Protein Mug Cake, 226, *227*
Vegan "Tuna" Casserole, *102*, 103–4
vegetables/veggies
  Chickpea and Veggie Pita Pockets, 94, *95*
  Feel-Good Roasted Red Pepper Veggie Soup, 140, *141*
  Minestrone Soup with a Twist, 125–27, *126–27*
  Parmesan Ratatouille, 118, *119*
  Veggie-Packed Lentil Rice Patties, 156–58, *157*
  Veggie Pot Pie Soup, 128–30, *129*

W
waffles
  Sweet Jalapeño Cornbread Waffles, *36*, 37
walnuts
  Chocolate Chip Walnut Protein Bars, 46–47, *47*

Y
yogurt (nondairy)
  Frozen Strawberry Yogurt Bark with Dark Chocolate, 234, *235*
  Lime Yogurt Chive Sauce, *254*, 255
  Swedish Gravy, 256, *257*

Z
zucchini
  Baked Zucchini Crisps, 210, *211*
  Comforting Sun-Dried Tomato and Zucchini Lasagna Soup, 144–46, *145*
  Parmesan Ratatouille, 118, *119*